DEDICATION

This book is dedicated[1] to all the congregants who worshipped God and served Christ in the community in this building since 1879 when the First Baptist of South Chicago was chartered[2]. Subsequently, it was a glorious day when these early English-speaking immigrants and first-generation Americans celebrated the opening of their House of God in 1885.

Similarly, this work is dedicated to the early immigrant, emigrants, and first-generation Mexicans who in 1926 established their Spanish-speaking in the building they co-shared the premises for almost three decades with the English-speaking Baptist congregation. The Mexican congregation used their initial name of *Primera Iglesia Bautista Mexicana de Sur Chicago* (First Mexican Baptist Church of South Chicago). In the 1930s, they changed their name to, *Iglesia Bautista El Salvador* (El Salvador Baptist Church).

In 1953, the First Baptist Church of South Chicago moved to another nearby neighborhood. Consequently, the Mexican Baptist congregation had the opportunity to purchase the building and one parcel of land and moved forward with God's providence. It changed its name again in a later years to *Primera Iglesia Bautista El Salvador.* Then in the 1960s, the Mexican Baptist Church changed its name to *Iglesia Bautista Del Salvador (*Del Salvador Baptist Church), which was its final name. This book is about these men and women and their work in South Chicago.

I am glad to have been able to find some scarce documentation about the history of the Mexican Baptist leaders, their ministry and activities. They were more than a singular sentence reference in the history of the Baptist work in South Chicago. Their history reveals how they struggled and succeeded in spreading the Gospel through their sixty-five year Christian ministry from 1926-1991 when it ceased its religious services as a congregation.

Their legacy is a glorious story of Believers representing men, women, children, and youth. They were unabashed for Christ in the challenging environs of South Chicago and nearby communities and other states. I was a humble servant here during some of these years and am honored to share this long overdue narrative.

THE FIRST BAPTIST CHURCH OF SOUTH CHICAGO

FACILITATOR IN ESTABLISHING THE FIRST MEXICAN BAPTIST CHURCH IN SOUTH CHICAGO

GEORGE BÉLOZ, Ph. D.

Includes Founding of Community Christian Church of Chicago

Trenton, Georgia

Copyright © 2024 George Béloz, Ph. D.

Print ISBN: 978-1-958890-16-5
Ebook ISBN: 979-8-88531-531-9

All rights reserved. No part of this publication may be reproduced, stored in a retrieval system, or transmitted in any form or by any means, electronic, mechanical, recording or otherwise, without the prior written permission of the author.

Published by BookLocker.com, Inc., Trenton, Georgia.

BookLocker.com, Inc.
2024

First Edition

Library of Congress Cataloging in Publication Data
Béloz, Ph. D., George
The First Baptist Church of South Chicago by George Béloz, Ph. D.
Library of Congress Control Number: 2023911403

THE FIRST BAPTIST CHURCH OF SOUTH CHICAGO

FACILITATOR IN ESTABLISHING THE FIRST MEXICAN BAPTIST CHURCH IN SOUTH CHICAGO

GEORGE BÉLOZ, Ph. D.

Includes Founding of Community Christian Church of Chicago

Contents

ACKNOWLEDGEMENTS 9
INTRODUCTION 11
PART I: FIRST BAPTIST CHURCH OF SOUTH CHICAGO 15
Founding (1879) 15
Early Photo of Building (circa 1885) 28
Pastors (1885-1953) 33
Move to a New Campus (1953) 36
The Cultural Institutions Research 38

PART II: THE FIRST MEXICAN BAPTIST CHURCH OF SOUTH
    CHICAGO (1926) 43
Historical References 45
Pastors of The Iglesia Bautista Del Salvador 1926-1991 50

PART III: MEXICANS PURCHASE THE BAPTIST BUILDING (1953) 55
Description of Building and Neighborhood 55
New Owners, Old Challenges 78
Membership Directories 82
Three Additional Land Parcels Bought (1965) 85
Building Signage 87
Interior Beautification 88
Interior Description 90
Entrance View 93
The Sanctuary Pulpit 103
Holy Communion Sacrament (*la Santa Cena*) 104
Baptism Sacrament 106
Music In the Services... 109
Christian Education 112
Sunday Morning Worship Services 117
Sunday Evening Services 119
Wednesday Evening Meetings 122
Additional Christian Education 123
Special Music Programs 124

A Good Friday Cantata 129
Other Choir Programs 133
Children in Music and Dramas 136
Beauty in Historic Houses of God 138

PART IV: LEADERSHIP AND DEVELOPMENT 143
Mexican Immigrants Choose South Chicago.. 143
Hispanic Leadership Recognition 153
Hispanic Baptist Conventions and Associations... 161
Presidents of The Convención Bautista Hispana-Americana
 1928-1978.. 164
Youth Activities 171

PART V: FOUNDING OF COMMUNITY CHRISTIAN CHURCH OF
 CHICAGO (1960)... 177
A Permanent Building Is Found (1988) 181
EPILOGUE 191
Notes About The Author 192
ABBREVIATIONS USED IN NOTES 193
NOTES... 195
BIBLIOGRAPHY 199
MEMBERS AND VETERANS OF IGLESIA BAUTISTA DEL SALVADOR........... 201
INDEX 203

ACKNOWLEDGEMENTS

There are many friends and members from *Iglesia Bautista Del Salvador*[3] who I met beginning in the mid-1950s and with whom I had the joy and pleasure of worshipping and working for Christ in this historic wooden building. Some were alive when I began gathering information and documentation about the history of this Spanish speaking congregation. One person was Mary Martínez, wife of Ramón Martínez. Little did I realize she had a trove of very early photographs and printed material about the people and activities starting in the early 1920s.

She and her daughter, Theresa Martínez, provided me photos and other material in the recent past. I received more items than I could have dreamed of and will share some of this material here. Mary left us suddenly before I could complete this work.

Another person who encouraged me from the outset was Amelia Balderas, wife of Rev. Efraín Balderas. Both were faithful leaders and servants in this and many other congregations throughout their lives in the Baptist faith. She offered historical information which was helpful. Similarly, like Mary, she, also recently left us for a better home after decades of Christian service.

I also must acknowledge Elisa Pérez, wife of Francisco (Frank) Pérez for providing me some photographs and Christian service programs I did not have in my files. Her constant inspiration to continue my effort is greatly appreciated. Frank left us in November 2023 while living in Chicago.

Another person I must thank is Sarah Montemayor Blasko. She provided me some material of the Baptist youth who grew up in this congregation who were slightly older than I as we worshiped together for some years. I lost contact with her shortly after I began this work.

I wish to greatly acknowledge my wife, Ruth, and my two daughters, Janet R. Stewart (Joseph), and Cheryl L. Morán (Ray) for their continuous encouragement for me to complete this work as I moved forward. My wife and young daughters were active in this church and worshipped in this historic Baptist building for many years. I also wish to thank all my friends who also encouraged me to write this story.

INTRODUCTION

The history of First Baptist Church of South Chicago and its relationship with the first Mexican Baptist congregation in this community is limited. I present the following history of their separate and intertwined story in Christian service.[4]

Part I discusses the history of the founding of the First Baptist Church of South Chicago in 1879, construction of its wooden structure in 1885, changes that took place in the building, and a brief history about some of its pastors.

Part II discusses how a group of Mexican immigrants sought assistance from two congregations and how the leadership in First Baptist Church of South Chicago facilitated the establishment of the first Mexican Baptist mission in 1926 within their building.

Part III discusses how in 1953, this nascent Christian body ultimately assumed ownership of the Baptist property, *Iglesia Bautista Del Salvador,* and its final name. We will learn about how they strove to beautify this House of God, its celebration of the Holy Sacraments, Sunday morning services and Sunday School. We will also discuss their Youth program, Wednesday mid-week services, and use of Christian music its regular and special programs.

Part IV discusses the impetus that brought the Mexican families to Chicago and established themselves in South Chicago from various states in México, and the U.S. states to ultimately plant the Spanish speaking Baptist mission in this area. We will also review the work of its leaders and congregants in the mid-1920s and how they launched a Spanish-language Baptist Association and Convention to combine their ministries to reach people for Christ for sixty-five years.

Part V discusses the history of the birth and growth of a new congregation, Community Christian Church of Chicago, which derived from *Iglesia Bautista Del Salvador* in 1960 and has continued its ministry for over sixty-four years.

My relationship with the Mexican Baptist congregation began sometime around 1954-1955 though I had learned about it in earlier years never thinking that I would become a member. I was welcomed by youth and older members. They encouraged me to consider becoming involved with this body and I did. Shortly thereafter, it changed its name to *Iglesia Bautista Del Salvador*. I will discuss its earlier names but generally will use this one throughout my narrative.

I believe throughout this congregation's history, the pastors and members of the Mexican congregation were adventurous leaders, eager, hardworking, and fearless as were the earlier European immigrant members of the First Baptist Church of South Chicago. The Spanish-speaking families sought to improve their employment, health, nutrition, education, and spiritual development as did the other ethnic groups that came to this community.

Similarly, they strove to acquire language skills in English while keeping active their own language and cultural activities. They established effective relationships with the community organizations, and quickly learned the social, educational, employment rules and regulations, social norms, laws and nuances of their dominant culture.

They faced many challenges from the first day they arrived in South Chicago. These endured for decades throughout this general community. Many professional, student historians, and sociologist have researched the Mexicans who settled in this area over one-hundred years. Until recently, insufficient history of and about the Mexican Baptist Spanish-speaking ministry has been published compared to other ethnic religious groups in South Chicago.

This book discusses some of the history as it relates to the above dynamic people who worshipped in this congregation. I will share some anecdotes and history of some of their experiences while we worshiped here. They were relentless and faithful men, women and youth who worked and served in many Baptist sponsored activities in and around South Chicago and other related organizations for sixty-five years as a congregation over one-hundred years as an ethnic group in this community. My story shares a small portion of them.

Facilitator in Establishing the First Mexican Baptist Church in South Chicago

My beginnings were in humble surroundings of immigrant parents who lived in a largely multi-immigrant community. This reality brought me and other first-generation sons and daughters born and raised in South Chicago some valuable experiences. These were meaningful opportunities from which we learned to overcome challenges with positive responses. Our leaders were pastors within *Iglesia Bautista Del Salvador* and others who served here as interim or ad hoc pastors. We experienced many Christian activities, educational programs in high school and university studies with some fine, wise, caring and encouraging people. I know this history is more extensive than what I am able to cover here. I hope other writers will continue where I end my effort and expand the history of these people and their Baptist work.

PART I:
FIRST BAPTIST CHURCH OF SOUTH CHICAGO

Founding (1879)

The history and development of the Christian Protestant ministry by the Baptist denomination in Chicago began in the October 18, 1833, when the First Baptist Church was founded on the north side of the city, the future downtown of Chicago.[5] This occurred four months after the Presbyterian denomination had organized, and two years after the Methodist church had formed in 1831. The First Baptist church's efforts to evangelize throughout Chicago continued for years after it was founded. Many extant Chicago Baptist churches can trace their roots to this mother church.

These roots run deep in history. These would include the First University of Chicago at 35th Street and Cottage Grove Avenue, Baptist Theological Union/University of Chicago Divinity School, Young Men's Christian Association, the Baptist Missionary Training School, other Baptist churches, and educational and community service centers as the South Chicago Neighborhood House which I discuss here.

These roots reached South Chicago residents and Baptist focused ministries directly or indirectly in various liaisons. It was through the efforts of their early leaders and of those who followed who believed in developing institutions of higher education, upholding Christ-like living, spreading the Gospel, and providing needed service to people of all ages that the Baptist ministry was brought to South Chicago.

The written history and activities of the First Baptist Church of South Chicago is not as prolific as the documented history of the First Baptist Church of Chicago. Nonetheless, the relationship between each exists. In my research of this relationship, in early 2019, I found a reference that states the First Baptist Church of South Chicago was chartered in 1879 in this Southeast part of Chicago. I was elated to learn about this date as it was almost unknown to many others nor to me when I tried to determine when the building was constructed in South Chicago. All we knew was that it was an old building.

When it received its charter, South Chicago did not exist as such. It was locally known as Ainsworth, a name derived from either a place in Brown County, Ireland, or the surname of an important Irish immigrant in this area. It was located within the expansive township of Hyde Park starting June 29, 1889, when South Chicago began.

It is one of the early Protestant churches in this area. It would make sense that this support derived from the mother Baptist Church in downtown and other Baptist organizations that existed to help nascent Baptist work advance in the City. Membership was probably not large but had potential in South Chicago which was a growing immigrant community. We learn that in 1901, its membership had grown substantially. Their charter began in South Chicago as this area was receiving increasing numbers of German, Swedish, Polish, Irish, and other Europeans. They began to arrive in this burgeoning place after the Civil War and during the decades between the 1870s and into the 1900s as is well documented.

It was the German and Swedish immigrants who were first drawn to this swampy terrain to live and work. They aspired to develop their spiritual needs as Baptists in America. It was they and other ethnic early immigrants who built the Baptist churches in South Chicago and a kaleidoscope of other ethnic denominational houses of prayer. Six years after receiving their charter, First Baptist Church of South Chicago announced it was seeking help as it moved forward with their building.

Inter Ocean newspaper out of Chicago, dated Sunday, February 2, 1885, briefly states, "The First Baptist Church of South is soliciting aid from other Baptist churches in the matter of a needed addition to their church edifice."[6] It would have been valuable to have information as to what the "addition" meant. The above article does not use the words "expanding" or "raising" which would clarify what was the excitement alluded to in this announcement.

Seven months later, in a brief article dated Saturday, September 19, 1885, *Inter Ocean* states that a dedication was to take place "one week from to-morrow," with the Rev. D.D. Odell as pastor.

Nine days later, in the *Chicago Tribune* article dated Monday, September 28, 1885, we read about the official "Church Dedication" service actually had taken place. It states, "The First Baptist Church of South Chicago was dedicated yesterday (Sunday)."[7] The dedication service was led by the congregation's pastor Rev. Odell, and four other distinguished visiting local Baptist pastors, and members and visitors who attended this weekend event. They came to participate in the dedicatory service of preaching and music in their new building. The article does not clearly confirm whether Pastor Odell is the first minister of this congregation. But it clearly states that "The Rev. Mr. Odell has done a good work in building up a church from a very humble beginning," strongly implying that he could have been in this position in 1879 when it was chartered. If so, he could be the first pastor of this congregation.

The Rev. Dr. Kennard of the Fourth Baptist Church, Chicago was invited to deliver the dedicatory message. The *Chicago Tribune* states that this sister congregation had provided the First Baptist Church of South Chicago "hearty support which had practically kept it alive during the dark times when the mills were idle and its members out of work." This was an early Baptist church on the West Side of the city.

Dr. Kennard's message was based on the Gospel of St. Matthew Chapter 26, Verse 42, about how Christ, "...because of His love for mankind and His knowledge that only by his shedding of His blood could the sins of the world be washed away." This was a powerful and encouraging message for the nascent congregation and to the developing community of South Chicago and environs in the 1800s. The newspaper article also informs us that, "The building is a pretty little frame structure, seating about 200 people...has been some time in building, but is now completely and nicely furnished," and is located at the corner of 90th and S. Houston Avenue. I have often wondered why it did not state the address as 9001 S. Houston Avenue. Perhaps my later discussion of this address difference will explain the variance.

The congregation's men may have built the building themselves. They must have spent months and even years receiving and unloading from horse-drawn wagons loaded with wood of different sizes and weights and other materials needed to build the structure. The region's winter and summer seasons during construction must have been very oppressive on the workers who probably volunteered their time, strength, and skills, as they became efficient in their tasks through on-the-job training. OSHA standards would not exist until at least one-hundred-eighty-seven years in the future.

If a worker was hired or volunteered and was injured, he just continued to work. He was minimally assisted at the site versus being taken by a horse drawn wagon to a nearby medical office. Workers brought their own lunch or enjoyed food the congregation's women may have brought them. Buying meals from fast-food drive-ins was unknown during 1883-1885 as the building was being constructed.

We also learn in the *Chicago Tribune* article of September 28, 1885, that the congregation is almost entirely made up of laborers and families who were barely surviving when the local rolling-mill was closed. The history of steel production industry began in the community of South Deering on July 5, 1875, ten years before the Baptist congregation dedicated their new House of God. The opening of the Joseph H. Brown Iron & Steel Company located nearby brought hundreds of new jobs to the immigrant laborers in their community.

I began attending Iglesia Bautista Del Salvador congregation in 1953-54. I always had an interest in learning as much as I could about the history of this building and its members. That is, information about the earliest English-speaking congregation and its leaders, its music, programs, and activities. I also wished to learn about how and when the Spanish-speaking congregation began to worship here. I was eager to gather information about the pastors of both congregations, and about their Christian ministry. I knew that finding answers would be a challenge and would take time to research.

One Saturday summer morning in the mid-1950s, soon after I was appointed organist of the Spanish-speaking congregation, I came to the building to practice the music for next day's service. After I finished, I decided to look in the back area of the building behind the baptistry where I had previously seen a small door which I assumed led to the attic. Looking up I saw it was at least eight feet above me. I remembered Jesús Gonsález had shown the men where long wooden ladders of different lengths were stored under the vaulted sidewalk on the west side of the building. He must have thought one day we would have use for them. That day, and occasion came for me.

I found and gave them a quick inspection and chose one that had a full set of steps and looked to be the most trustworthy. Being a young strong man, I carried it up the interior of the building's back stairway and brought it to the attic door.

I anticipated discovering historic documents: books, financial ledgers, photographs, newspapers, money, or nothing as is often found in the attics of old buildings. Opening the door carefully, I saw the wooden inner beams that supported the ceiling of the sanctuary below and the framework of the roof. I dared not enter this area for fear of falling into the sanctuary. The attic was fully covered with decades of thick, grey, dry dust. Visually scanning the expansive attic. I saw no boxes and I was baffled.

But, just a few feet below the door opening, I saw three dust covered documents scattered one on top of each other and part of a third pamphlet. I leaned over the opening and was able to safely retrieve them without falling into the attic. Picking them up, I saw they were professionally printed paper booklets. I was anxious to see what these items were, how old they might be, and what information they contained. Based on the dust on them, they appeared to have been lying in this area for decades. The dates on the items would reveal this information but not how long they had been deposited here.

The first item was a copy of the ninety-year-old, *The South Chicago Baptist Review, Thanksgiving Number, November 1928*.[8] The First Baptist Church of South Chicago published it one month after the start of Great Depression. The Financial Report indicated that income was $416 ($12,350 in current value), and $352 ($6,000 today) had been spent during that period. It also states, "Our Sunday School is growing...and had 122 last Sunday. Church services are well attended, a full house every Sunday night." Some interesting articles provide various non-faith statistics for pre-or post-prohibition era days.

In a paid advertisement in the *Review*, the funeral directors of a local business, Adam Griesel & Son announced, "Complete Adult Funerals $98.00" ($8,000 average in Chicago today). No photographs are found in this publication. It lists the congregation's pastor, Rev. Martin L. Long, church clerk, Mrs. Jonnie Lane, and financial secretary, Frank A. Gifford. Their personal home and telephone numbers, in the *Regent* or *South Chicago* prefix, are listed as well.

The second item was an article in the *Review* from Thursday, October 10, 1929.[9] It indicates that a team from the First Baptist Church of South Chicago would be presenting a program that evening. The choir was to sing "tonight at the 10:15 o'clock" at the campus of Moody Bible Institute's nascent radio program, WMBI, which was located on the Northwest Side of Chicago. Their pastor Rev. Long was to bring the message. Apparently, these Baptist services ran long into the night which was common in stalwart Baptist congregations.

If this were a live performance, the Baptist team had to have taken hours that day to travel to and from this station. They were resolute choristers, nineteen days before the Great Depression began. The phonograph had already been invented but the tape recorder was not until 1948. What a treasure we would have today if they had recorded their entire program.

We read the congregation's total treasury balance in 1929 was around sixty-five dollars ($1,166 today), they had low membership and attendance, and some unpaid expenses were due.

The third item I retrieved from the attic was published three years after the one mentioned above. This is the twenty-eight-year-old, *Illinois Baptist Bulletin, Vol. XXIII, No. 12, June 1932, Joliet, Illinois*.[10] This publication provides information about state-wide Northern Baptist Convention activities, an organization with which the First Baptist Church of South Chicago was probably a member. It also contained articles about the church's activities, poems submitted by members, the pastor's mini-lesson, and some information about the financial status of the congregation.

A story in the above publication about Northern Baptists twenty-fifth Convention in San Francisco, July 12-17, states, "The hope and expectation seems to be general that, from a spiritual standpoint, it is to be the greatest convention the denomination has ever held." The Convention's theme was, "Shall we be Christians?" Interestingly, two publications from the mid-1920s reveal the Spanish-speaking Baptist Convention and Associations were involved in similar meetings for their members during this same period. I will discuss these later.

In the *Daily Times* of Chicago, dated January 13, 1931, I found a biblical article which Rev. Long had submitted.[11] It was based on Psalm chapter 27, verse 1: "The Lord is my light and my salvation; whom shall I fear? the Lord is the strength of my life; of whom shall I be afraid?" The references about this pastor and the congregation's activities indicate that South Chicago Baptist Church was actively moving forward their Christian message of encouragement and hope through means of print and the use of the air waves to reach a grater audience through WMBI radio. If we could locate references to these activities, I believe information about this congregation's pastors and their work would be replete with the history of their work in South Chicago and elsewhere and how they delivered the *Good News*.

One day during one of my visits to Chicago, probably in the fall of 2015, I went to the Southeast Chicago Historical Society museum, a local area history repository located in Calumet Park Field House. I thought here I would find a trove of articles and documents about the First Baptist Church of South Chicago. I inquired about information they might have in their archives. To my chagrin, I found limited material, other than a note which stated that Rev. Kelly was pastor in 1899. This was fourteen years after the First Baptist Church of South Chicago had been constructed in 1885. It could be he was their second pastor who followed the founding pastor Rev. Odell as I have listed on roster of pastors I present here.

Sometime in 2020, as I continued to search for critical data about this congregation I acquired a valuable source.[12] This research was conducted by Dr. John M. Gillette (1866-1949), titled, *The Cultural Agencies of a Typical Manufacturing Group: South Chicago, Illinois*.[13] It provides data about First Baptist Church in South Chicago in 1901. In Chapter II, Cultural Agencies, Section I, Religious Agencies, we learn that this congregation had a membership of 235 on their rolls.

Dr. Gillette's research states that First Baptist Church of South Chicago continued to have an English class to meet the needs of some fifty German limited-English speakers and the rest of the members were now chiefly speaking English and others were American families. South Chicago's congregation was one of two Baptist churches in this community. The other was composed entirely of Swedish ancestry members. Gillette notes that there are six other German nationality congregations who were also active in the area including Methodist and other ethnic congregations as they spread the Gospel throughout the community.

The First Baptist Church of South Chicago was an independent religious entity. It was generally self-sustaining, operated under its own By-Laws, maintained a Christian Baptist teaching philosophy, selected its own pastor, and managed its local financial budget. It had to be spiritually strong and focused on its message of personal salvation through Christ, the Holy sacraments of baptism by total immersion in water, celebrating the Holy Communion and being a witness for Christ to everyone. I will discuss this subject later in this text.

I would not be surprised if First Baptist Church of Chicago assisted First Baptist Church of South Chicago in spiritual guidance, leadership training, and financial support. However, Dr. Gillette's study does not discuss these topics.

I could not confirm whether First Baptist Church of South Chicago was debt free or the size of their mortgage in its beginning. More than likely, it had a long-term mortgage. It is possible that it had other private business agreements with lenders to purchase furniture for the sanctuary and all the other rooms or to cover other expenses as they opened their new building. I imagine the floors were made of simple oak planks sans carpeting.

In a 1964 letter[14] written to Rev. Ralph Sanderson, the director of the South Chicago Neighborhood House, confirms First Baptist Church of South Chicago established this center in the *Bush* community 1914. Also, a 1982 reprint[15] from *NUESTRO Magazine* (*Our Magazine*), states a "local Baptist church" also supports Sanderson's statement. I feel confident to say that the First Baptist Church of Chicago was the "local" partner alluded to in this article. If we had the congregation's Charter, I believe we would see this type of activity was one of their goal statements.

Jack Paul Rocha provides a synopsis of this center's history in the April 2022 *Southeast Chicago Historical Society News*.[16] The community center focused on the spiritual and secular interests of people living in the *Bush* neighborhood. South Chicago Baptist Church principally focused on the people's spiritual needs but also helped in other needs as well. Both organizations were constant in their efforts to serve people. The building has been closed but is extant.

Strong working bonds between these two Baptist organizations brought a myriad of programs. They historically assisted the earlier immigrants and those in transition who lived in this precarious highly densely populated blue collar industrial community.

Influential local iron and steel businessmen such as Col. James H. Bowen, and John H. Brown and other leaders were launching exciting plans to bring major economic development to South Chicago when First Baptist Church of South Chicago was beginning. The early history is documented of how these two men brought thousands of jobs to

South Chicago which would employ the immigrants who were already here and were continuing to arrive.

The history of jobs in iron and steel production in the area began almost 150 years ago. On July 5, 1875, Mr. John H. Brown, Col. James H. Bowen, and other local leaders ceremoniously opened the John H. Brown Iron and Steel Company on some one-hundred acres of land donated by Col. Bowen. The enterprise was located along the shores of the Calumet River just south and west of where the future Baptist house of worship was going to be built just six years hence. Local residents, mostly immigrant men, would find employment in the nascent steelmaking industry for decades.

In 1881, another steel making company began operations. It was the North Chicago Rolling Mill Company which started to meet the demands for more steel in Chicago and across the nation. In later years this company, South Works, was located near the foot of East 91st Street on less than seventy-five acres along the shores of Lake Michigan next to the Calumet River. This Lake was a major factor in facilitating the company's future needs to receive ships bringing the basic steel-making elements to the mills and the ease in shipping a myriad of finished steel products to their buyers. South Works was closer than the Brown Iron and Steel Company. Its first steel rail was manufactured in the summer of 1882 which was a major industrial invention by replacing rail tracks made of iron.

While the company manufactured other metal products such as nails for building barns and houses and other metal products, steel production alone could meet the high demand of the railroad industry which was expanding throughout the country. It required thousands of men from this the local area. Despite being in the heart of a nascent industrial zone, South Works suffered unsustainable revenue losses and had to make tough management decisions.

An article in *Chicago Tribune*, dated Wednesday, December 13, 1882, states that the president of the North Chicago Steel Company, Orrin W. Potter, became upset during an interview in his office with a newspaper reporter who asked why the South Chicago plant had recently been shut down.[17] Mr. Potter replied closing this neighborhood plant was not due to the worker's strike but was because the price of labor was too expensive to keep the overall North and South mills open. He could not provide a date as to when the mill would reopen and only responded, "This is about all I wish to say on the subject, as it has already been fully discussed," and the meeting ended.

This closing must have impacted the Baptist congregation's workers and all who worked in the mill. For the former group, their income fell just as the planning and construction progressed on their building. Employment and worker's wages at the South Chicago plant were perennial issues which steelworkers had to contend with at this time and throughout the future history of worker's struggle to survive.

On April 10, 1992, one hundred years after having opened its doors this industry closed forever. I remember it was known by various names: Carnegie Steel, Illinois Steel, US Steel, South Works, and ultimately USX. A comprehensive narrative and pictorial history of this company is found in the book by Rod Sellers, *Chicago's Southeast Side Industrial History*. Over these decades of operating, it expanded its footprint to just under six-hundred acres of land, which included reclaimed Lake Michigan's beach beginning at 79th Street, to 92nd Street for some thirteen blocks north and south, and half a mile east and west. The mill complex could be seen by all who travelled through the area.

This steel manufacturing industry provided millions of workers employment over its lifetime. It permanently closed its doors and displaced its last seven hundred workers who were still employed at this time. It was an historic and dominant factor in the development of the South Chicago area and worldwide. Its steel products were used to build bridges, building superstructures, piers, railroad tracks, and meeting the demands for war materiel during its existence. It was a giant which left its good and bad footprint for decades.

There were other labor-intensive industries where some members of the First Baptist Church of South Chicago may have worked. These included coal yards, major railroad yards, shipyards along the Calumet River receiving and shipping tons of products in and out of the area, and lumber company docks along the Calumet River and the Strand area near the river. Local newspapers published daily schedules and details about industrial sailboat and steamboat manifests that were arriving in local rivers and docks. It is possible some of the men from the Baptist congregation worked at Col. Bowen's earlier corporation The Calumet & Chicago Canal & Dock Company which opened in 1870 along the Calumet River. Hundreds of men worked in this burgeoning industry for decades. All of these companies were near to the Baptist's campus. We can only speculate as to where these men worked beyond the "rolling mills" as mentioned in the September 28, 1885, *Chicago Tribune* article.

Despite the unfavorable economic conditions in the country and throughout South Chicago, the Baptist building was dedicated six years after receiving their Charter in 1879 from the State of Illinois, and probably some financial and spiritual support from the Baptist organizations in Chicago. This historic milestone involved a major decision, beginning with the purchase of two contiguous parcels of slough and prairie land sited above and other parcels which we will discuss later in this text. They had great confidence in their God and in themselves.

Boldly, they moved forward with excitement to succeed and were guided by God's still, small, voice, the wisdom of their leaders, and congregant's spiritual, financial and other support. Their decisions were challenging. They had to seek and meet goals concerned with financial, in-kind contributions, planning and designing the building's parameters and construction timetables, in order to be able to have a "complete and nicely furnished" building to inaugurate it as described in the *Chicago Tribune* article of September 1885.

Other congregation information and data is not referenced in the above *Chicago Tribune* article. It does not tell us the price they paid for the property nor the value of the structure, or who designed this simple 19th century building. Answers to these topics will require future research.

Also, the above article did not state how many years it took to complete the edifice. It could have taken a couple of years, if the congregation men did most of the work themselves. We do not know if the lancet windows were mounted with stained glass. Though photography was available in 1888, I have not found any pictures of the building as it was under construction. The one I have may have been taken shortly after it was completed though it is devoid of a crowd of observers as is seen when new buildings are inaugurated .

As European and American born families arrived in the area, they came along or brought their families with them. This created a need for classrooms to educate the youth. In time, the first small wood-frame one-story elementary school building was constructed on land where the extant South Chicago Fire Department building is located at South 93rd Street between Commercial Avenue and S. Houston Avenue.

In order to meet the increasing classroom need, in 1876 a larger and new majestic two-story hewn stone and brick building with a large attic was constructed to replace the first schoolhouse. It was located on the west side of 93rd Street and S. Houston Avenue. It was named the South Chicago Grammar School. This building was located just two blocks south on S. Houston Avenue where the Baptist would build their house of worship in 1885.

School enrollment increased as South Chicago's American born and immigrant school-age cohorts continued to grow. They needed education programs to prepare them beyond the common grammar school level. In 1882 a portion of the attic area of grammar school building was repurposed by the Chicago Board of Education and the local parents' demand. The action began the start of the original Bowen High School studies for South Chicago's youth. In 1888, an extension was added to the original one to meet the continuing demand in primary and secondary education.

In this same year, two other nearby public elementary schools were constructed who were also facing the growing student enrollment of the same backgrounds as Bowen's. They were James N. Thorp, and Philip H. Sheridan elementary schools. Both are extant today. I knew several students who were members of *Iglesia Bautista Del Salvador* and were enrolled in each of these.

The only comprehensive history of Bowen High School[18] can be found in a Sixth Edition I self-published in 2018 titled, *Colonel James Harvey Bowen: The Epic of His Life and South Chicago's First High School Centennial Celebration*. A copy of this item may be found in Chicago, Illinois: *Southeast Chicago Historical Society Cultural Center* in Calumet Park field house, South Chicago Public Library, and Hegewisch Public Library. Also three locations in California: Corona Public Library, Cypress College Library Special Collections, and Home Gardens Public Library near Corona. First and second editions were also available at various Bowen High School alumni reunions.

Early Photo of Building (circa 1885)

As I continued my research as to when the First Baptist of South Chicago building was constructed, I looked at building addresses of other church buildings in South Chicago.[19] My results were unfruitful as they had no actual dates for any houses of worship. However, many non-religious building construction dates were readily available. It was a conundrum. However, in 2020-2021, as the COVID-19 was ravaging the world, I accessed on-line newspaper articles and other sources which provided information related to the activities of the First Baptist Church of South Chicago.

I learned the First Baptist Church building of South Chicago was built in 1885, twenty years after the U.S. Civil War ended. It has been a dominant structure at the corner of 9001 S. Houston Avenue since construction. It is located one block east of Commercial Avenue, one block east of Exchange Avenue, and two blocks south on 92nd Steet.

It is within a quarter-of-a-mile west of the magnificent Lake Michigan, and some eleven miles southeast of downtown Chicago.

We are able to see and describe what the original building[20] looked like on a particular day from an historic photograph I received in mid-February 2021. A handwritten notation on it by someone states, "Babtist [sic] Church—So. Chicago." It is undated with this misspelling in the name as it might have been spoken and written by some the local residents. The sepia photograph provides a configuration of the exterior previously unknown to me and probably many others during the 19th-21st centuries.

We see a one-storied wooden building with a basement. I surmise it dates from 1885, shortly after it was completed. The original building was slightly shorter on its north end before the extension of some ten feet of concrete blocks was added. I have no date when this occurred. This could have happened along with the other building modifications when the building was raised before 1895 or thereafter when other changes took place. A twenty-foot shiplap wooden campanile tower is seen in the photograph. It protrudes near the roof on the northwest corner of the building. We do not know if it ever housed any bells or was only an architectural design to the edifice.

The tower had two short windows facing west, just below the louvered opening facing the same direction near the top of the sharp apex of the tower. Another louvered opening faces north just under the eaves of the lower end of the tower roof. Medium sized width wooden fascia cover the roof rafters and other portions of the building. We have no information as to how many years the tower existed before it was removed. It was gone before the mid-1950s.

In the building's original design, people would enter the sanctuary from the wooden planked public sidewalk that surrounded it along S. Houston Avenue and along S. 90th Street. They would walk up a ten-foot wooden staircase located at the north facing corner of the building. People could also enter it through the basement doorway at ground elevation on S. Houston Avenue frontage of the building, or any other basement entrance not seen in the photo.

On the S. Houston Avenue side of the basement's west wall is a door and six long lancet styled windows, appearing to be slightly smaller than the five windows on the upper part of the building's wall where the sanctuary area was located. We see a small lancet window in the entryway's north wall and another one just below it on S. 90th Street. A double-doored entrance to the sanctuary on the upper floor is seen. A small barely visible wooden rectangular sign is seen on the corner of S. 90th Street and S. Houston Avenue. It is where all future announcement signs will be attached to the exterior wall by both Baptist Churches and other future churches that occupied the building.

Along the upper north wall we see four lancet styled shaped windows. One is under the right side of the roof eaves. Here we see a group of people looking at whoever was taking the photo. We also see three windows in the same style: one at the first-floor level to the right of the entrance, and one in the small lobby of the entrance, and one in the basement area of the building.

There is an enclosed porch-like entrance with a short, slanted roof leading into the building. Four women wearing long dresses stand at the top of the stairs and four others at the bottom. A young boy stands near the bottom of the stairs just ahead of them, and another one is on the wooden sidewalk just before the stairs.

There is a man standing on the wide planked wooden sidewalk looking eastward at the building. He is dressed in a dark overcoat and wearing what appears to be a Stetson wool Fedora hat. Based on apparel worn by the boys and this adult man, the photo seems to have been taken in the fall or winter season in South Chicago. It is possible that this person might be the first Pastor, Rev. D.D. Odell (1885-), or his successor, Rev. A.C. Kelly (1894-1899), depending on the year when the photo was taken.

At the back left top of the roof, we barely see a small portion of the brick chimney emerging. It was used for the passage of smoke from the stoves that heated the basement, sanctuary, and other interior rooms. They probably burned coal, coke, or wood as fuel.

Based on the location of the chimney seen in the photo, a big iron stove (heater) may have been located in the middle of the sanctuary and another one in the basement. The stoves were hand fed as whole-house heating systems were not commonly found in most buildings when this photo was taken. The building may have used any of the above fuels to heat the stoves which provided heat to the rooms. Or a boiling water system with iron radiators throughout the building. However, I believe this kind of system came later when the building was modified and raised.

The left side of the photo reveals what was probably unknown information to many people. It is about the existence of a structure immediately on the east side of the building. I have never seen any artifacts of a building's foundation on this parcel. In the photo we see a limited portion of the side of a building and its slanted roof next to the church structure.

The residential building appears to have been two-storied. It was probably owned by the congregation. It could have been the residence where the pastor and family lived. This convenience was commonly provided to pastors as part of their compensation then and today. In time, the structure was demolished though we have no information as to when this occurred. The land remained vacant for many decades. The lot is seen in 1897 Sanborn Fire Insurance Map discussed later in this book.

We have no information regarding the dates of this change and the others that are discussed herein. The building was elevated some eight-to-ten additional feet to its current height using concrete block. The extension provided a new double-door entrance to the building's north profile on S. Houston Avenue and was capped by a stone lintel. This extension provided additional square footage to the basement and first floor including a higher ceiling and overall height of the building.

I remember seeing two or three massive square support beams that were in the ceiling of the basement. They were probably added when the building was raised to strengthen the integrity of the floor above and the building itself. These were observable for decades and probably replaced with new beams by current owners in the early 2020s. The basement's original arched window modifications help us compare the earlier photo to later ones. The new level and width of the concrete sidewalks around the structure changed the exterior appearance of the building slightly.

The extension on the north part of the roof and wall facing the east were modified using concrete block walls versus continuing to use wood. Three new clear windowpanes brought in more light into this room under the roof facing east and north. Also, three small, lancet styled stain-glass windows were part of the extension.

Similar changes were made to the south doorway entrance and the lintel almost matching the north entrance, but without any half-moon arched window and any smaller ones.

I have not found any photographs of the appearance of the original interior rooms of the building. I photographed the sanctuary as it appeared when I was a member of *Iglesia Bautista Del Salvador,* and I describe it as it might have looked in early years. A small room on the southwest corner wall behind the sanctuary was part of the original building. Its external view is seen in the historic photograph. It may have been used as an office. This section was removed and modified when the building was redesigned. The Spanish-speaking church used this room as the pastor's office and often for a Sunday School room.

Though the pews I saw in the sanctuary appear to be original, without photos, it is difficult to determine if they are from 1885 or later. The oak wood floor in the sanctuary appeared to be original. The exterior window frames were probably original but could have been modified somewhat in later years. Ten lancet stained-glass windows on the first floor were in situ in 1953 when *Iglesia Bautista Del Salvador* purchased it. These were removed during a remodeling project in the late 1960s. This action marked the beginning of a new view of the interior of the sanctuary and entire outside of the east and west walls. This topic is discussed elsewhere in this book.

Also, we have no information about the original interior lighting system that was used in the building. These were probably decorated by fixtures that burned natural gas and had to be hand-lit when illumination was needed beyond the natural light that entered through the windows in the first floor, basement, or in the small attic located under the original roof on the north side of the building.

Pastors (1885-1953)

As I have previously stated, First Baptist Church of South Chicago was chartered in 1879 and served at 90th and S. Houston Avenue for seventy-four years in the small wood-frame building built in 1885 before it moved to a new brick structure on Merrill Avenue. I have always been interested in learning about this congregation, its pastors, and about its Christian service to the community. This was not a simple task. I wished to prepare a list of First Baptist Church of South Chicago pastors between 1885-1953, who served at the Houston Avenue address. I found brief information from various sources.

These include newspapers and a variety of sources. One was *Illinois Baptist Church Directory,* Baptist Church monthly journals, and local church publications from the 19th and 20th centuries. Photos of the pastors are rare except for one which contained a picture of Rev. Thompson in a local newspaper. I could not confirm the actual tenure dates of when the pastors served here. The dates I have written after each name is the year(s) when they are referenced in an article or journal about their ministry starting when the building was dedicated in 1885 up to the year in which the congregation moved to 9100 S. Merrill Avenue, in 1953.

Pastors of First Baptist Church of South Chicago (1885-1953)[21]

Rev. D. D. Odell, 1885
Rev. A. C. Kelly, 1894-1899

Rev. Cotton, 1923
Rev. Edgar Woolhouse, 1925

Rev. J. W. T. McNeill, 1902   Rev. Martin Long, 1929
Rev. C. F. Vreeland, 1905   Rev. Dre. William C. Boyd, 1938
Rev. A. A. Mohoney, 1905   Rev. Henry Thompson, 1953

An additional minister, Rev. Harry E. Cochenour, is listed on the church's 1964 stationery, as pastor of this congregation located at the Merrill Avenue address. I have no date as to this succession. Nor do I have information about other pastors thereafter until 2021. This is when I leaned that the congregation had moved to a new property and taken on a new name, Compassion Baptist Church of Chicago, and a led by pastor Rev. Watson Jones III.

The sources I found provide brief information about what these pastors were doing at particular activities. Early in 2021 Rod Sellers provided me two names I did not have and I added these to the ones I had previously gleaned.

I found no information regarding any non-preaching employment which the English-speaking pastors may have had. Other employment would not have been unusual considering the congregation was small and had a limited annual budget to support them. Several pastors in the Spanish-speaking congregation we discuss later in this book were employed elsewhere to sustain himself and his family.

The ministers were principally busy preaching, teaching, and carrying out their Christian work assignments with youth and the other congregants. Some were actively involved in leading area-wide Baptist activities in other similar congregations and Christian studies institutions. It appears that some of these men were well prepared to serve Christ and the community during their tenures.

Pastor Dr. Boyd earned a doctorate degree during his ministerial preparation. It could have been in theology or preaching. Under his leadership, First Baptist Church of South Chicago hosted a series of studies that focused on prayer, Bible conference[22], and youth outreach services. In the *Evening Star*, of Saturday, August 30, 1902, we learn about pastor McNeil. He was born in Virginia in 1873. He is reported to have been a recognized pastor and evangelist in a small church in the local area where he lived but its name is not provided.

He married Annie S. Goodloe in 1900 in Gordonsville, Virginia. The couple moved to Chicago where they both enrolled in the nascent University of Chicago to complete their studies. Annie suddenly died in 1901. He continued his studies and completed these in June 1902. The article tells us he thereafter "supplied the pulpit of First Baptist Church of South Chicago," without providing any further information. His assignment was probably through the Chicago Baptist Association in conjunction with the local church's approval as was the general process then and for years thereafter.

The 1900 *Chicago Lakeside City Directory of Churches* lists the name[23] of this congregation but does not indicate the name of the pastor. In 1905, another source indicates that there were sixty-five Baptist churches in Chicago. First Baptist Church of South Chicago lists pastor Vreeland as its minister. Interestingly, the *Chicago Directory Company of 1905* of churches reveals that Rev. Mohney is also listed at the pastor here, which is why two pastors' names are listed above in the same year. It would be a treasure trove to us if we could find the preaching notes used by any of these pastors while they served in South Chicago and elsewhere.

It would be interesting to have historical information about the language abilities the pastors may have had and used, especially in the early years of this congregation. Certainly, they used English, but we must remember this community was comprised of thousands of immigrants who arrived in South Chicago and used their native language. As they acculturated and became first-generation U.S. citizens, they slowly transitioned into speaking more English and less of their mother tongue.

I am only aware of the photograph of one pastor out of the eleven of First Baptist Church of South Chicago before they moved. I would not be surprised that some of the early pastors sported well-kempt beards and mustaches commensurate with the eras in which they served here. I found a facsimile of Rev. Thompson[24] which appeared on February 3, 1953, on the front page of The *Daily Calumet Newspaper*. He was a bespectacled, seemingly tall, clean-shaven thin person in the prime of his life. In the article he shares his belief about being a Christian as said earlier. He reflects an exuberant spirit ready to lead the congregation forward as it was preparing to move to their new campus in a new neighborhood just west of South Chicago.

Move to a New Campus (1953)

The First Baptist Church of South Chicago and its English-speaking congregation moved in 1953 to a new community. Their new, small brick structure was built at the southwest corner of 91st and S. Merrill Avenue. First Baptist Church of South Chicago, under Rev. Henry Thompson renamed itself, Merrill Avenue Baptist Church. It was now located in the community of Calumet Heights, also called, "Pill Hill," alluding to the number of medical doctors and other staff who lived and worked at the nearby former South Chicago Hospital and lived in this community. The Merrill Avenue campus was located just a few miles west of S. Houston Avenue.

An article and picture[25] in the *Daily Calumet* dated Monday, February 2, 1953, announced the dedication of the ground and the foundation of the site where the new brick building was going to be located. The article does not tell us whether a cornerstone was placed at this time. A picture of Pastor Thompson shows him as he stands behind a lectern of the walless building. He is surrounded by congregants and visitors, including Rev. Basil Williams of South Chicago Neighborhood House in the *Bush* community.

New impressive homes were displacing obsolete factories in the Calumet Heights neighborhood. Demographics were shifting and young white-collar workers were building large homes which resulted in a solidly middle-class community. Congregation members begun to move into this community with some coming from South Chicago. The congregation served God and the community on Merrill Avenue for fifty-eight years (1953-2011).

Facilitator in Establishing the First Mexican Baptist Church in South Chicago

During these years, it continued to experience new changes in its ministry. A major one for Merrill Avenue Baptist Church was the new demographics of the community which was occurring throughout the greater South Chicago area. As more African American families moved into this community, they were attracted here as their income increased and some sought a Baptist house of worship close to home. In time, they became the new majority congregants as older members died or moved away.

Probably after much consideration, discussion, planning, and prayer, the leaders and members of this congregation sought and acquired a larger piece of vacant property on which they would build a new and larger brick house of worship. In August 2011, Merrill Avenue Baptist Church moved to another new campus. They changed their name to, Compassion Baptist Church of Chicago before or after they moved. This name expresses the essence of their Christian mission. It is fully Christ-led and prepared to deliver its message to this community and surrounding environs, even reaching into nearby Indiana communities as stated in their webpage.

The new site is located at 2650 E. 95th Street, near S. Colfax Avenue, Chicago, southwest of their former Merrill Avenue address. Their website in 2020 indicates its pastor is Rev. Watson Jones III, and his supportive wife, Kelli, and their three children, Yeshaya, Watson IV, and Ellison. I believe Pastor Jones may have succeeded Pastor Thompson, who served at this campus from 1953 until an unknown date.

The exterior façade of the building displays a contemporary look throughout, with ample car parking on its property. Its interior is also a beautiful compliment for this house of worship in terms of interior natural sunlight, beautiful sanctuary and appointments, which I have only seen on their webpage and a brief exterior visit in early 2023. Other amenities include a baptistry, classrooms, and a Christian academy on its campus which indicates its support of Christian education for youth.

Today, the congregation is totally African American and comprised of all generations of men, women, children, and youth. Its leadership and congregation are determined to remain within the Baptist beliefs and practices as they continue their mission to reach people with a compassionate and Christian focus in all its services and programs.

Its website proudly traces its Christian history to the First Baptist Church of South Chicago. This is a clear direct linkage to one-hundred-and-forty-one years of active Baptist ministry which started in the very heart of South Chicago by European immigrants.

The Cultural Institutions Research

While in Chicago on October 1, 2015, I visited the Southeast Chicago Historical Museum to research First Baptist Church of South Chicago, and *Iglesia Bautista Del Salvador*. While here, I acquired a copy[26] of *Chicago's Southeast Side Cultural Institutions: A Community of Churches*. I kept it as I found its content very informative. In 2020, during a conversation with Joann Podkul, I learned that she had assisted high school teacher and Project Coordinator, Rod Sellers and another teacher Ken O'Neal in writing a grant proposal to the Southeast Historical museum to fund a cultural study class to research South Chicago's houses of worship.

Their proposal was accepted between 2002-2004 at a minimal grant amount from the Oppenheimer Family Foundation and Disney Creative Classroom Grant, through the Chicago Board of Education channels. The study was prepared in after-class hours by a group of some twenty extraordinary Washington High School students on the premises of the Southeast Chicago Historical Society Cultural Center in Calumet Park Field House and the school.

The study is valuable because it shares historical summaries of Christian and one Jewish congregation that were established in the area. However, it lacks information about First Baptist Church of South Chicago or the work of the Mexican Baptists. It does, however, briefly discuss the founding of the Spanish-speaking Our Lady of Guadalupe

Church to serve the Mexican Roman Catholic population here at its original location on 90th and S. Mackinaw Avenue.

I learned an explanation from one of the leaders of the high school study why information about the two Baptist congregations was missing. One reason may be because the English-speaking Baptist had moved out of the building in 1953 after having occupied it for sixty-eight years.

Once they moved, if they were contacted perhaps their interests waned in providing information they may have had in their archives. Or the Spanish-speaking Baptist congregation, who had co-occupied the building with the First Baptist Church of South Chicago between 1926-1953, and then as full owners between 1953-1991, had already closed its activities here.

The leaders of either congregation may not have perceived the letter as important. Or perhaps they found it inconvenient or unrealistic for them to reply; or perhaps they did not receive it at all. I am not aware if other contacts were attempted, e.g., telephone calls or personal visits. As a result, the research project was void of data.

However, the Museology Class contributed valuable paragraphs about the history of Our Lady of Guadalupe Catholic Church, a basically Spanish-speaking parish. I believe it is important to briefly share additional history about how both the Mexican Catholic population and the Mexican Baptists began to deliver the Gospel within blocks of each other in this very ethnic industrial working-class area in the mid-to late 1920s.

Our Lady of Guadalupe Catholic Church is the oldest Mexican Catholic Spanish-speaking parish in Chicago. It was started and founded under the leadership of Father William Kane, S.J. to meet the spiritual and social needs of the expanding immigrant Mexican population in South Chicago. Through his efforts in 1924, a small wood frame barracks[27] (probably from a former military camp) in Southern Michigan was brought to 9024 S. Mackinaw Avenue. As a youth I remember walking or riding my bicycle past this unmarked vacant site for years. I knew nothing about the humble building that once existed here nor about its history, inspiring leaders or Mexican worshippers. Its history was forgotten and neither my parents nor paternal relatives shared information with me about this early house of God.

The wood bungalow was soon modified into a house of worship. Their first pastor was Father John Maizteguí, a Claretian priest. In 1926, a larger piece of property was acquired (donated or purchased) at 91st and S. Brandon Avenue. After vigorous years of ministering by the Catholic leaders and parishioners' efforts, on Sunday, September 30, 1928, Mexican Catholics dedicated and laid the cornerstone of their new three-storied brick and steel house of worship, constructed in the Italian Renaissance revival architectural design.

Cardinal George William Mundelein, Archbishop of Chicago, dedicated the building. My family had an historic photograph of this event. I was told that my widowed grandmother, her three sons and daughter were present at this event. One of these sons became my father just ten years in the future. More about this house of worship is discussed later in this book.

On February 17, 1929, Saint Jude Shrine "patron of difficult and hopeless cases," celebrated its inaugural Solemn Novena, a nine-day period of attentive prayers thanking God for this new building. Both institutions are extant and active in 2024 as they continue to serve the Catholic Latino and other Catholic populations from the area and elsewhere for regular services and Novenas.

In late 2017, I bought a book on-line[28] titled, *Spires of Faith, Historic Churches of Chicago*. It was a discarded holding from a regional Chicago Public Library. It contains information and pictures about forty-one beautiful extant and razed Catholic Church buildings located throughout Chicago, before and after the Great Chicago Fire of 1871. Nothing in it helped my research about the Baptist building in South Chicago. I realized this was because the document only focused on the kaleidoscope trove of beautiful Catholic Church buildings in our fair city and not on Protestant houses of worship.

I was also surprised to learn information about three magnificent Catholic houses of worship located in South Chicago is missing in this book. These are: Saint Michael Archangel Roman Catholic Church (1909), at 8237 S. South Shore Drive, the Immaculate Conception Catholic Church (1899), 2944 E. 88th Street and Commercial Avenue, and Our Lady of Guadalupe Church (1928) at 3200 E. 91st Street. Nothing is mentioned about them in the footnotes, nor in the beautiful twenty-five pencil sketches at the back of the book where other extant and former houses of worship are drawn.

PART II:
THE FIRST MEXICAN BAPTIST CHURCH OF SOUTH CHICAGO (1926)

Extensive histories of older congregations and other houses of worship in South Chicago seem to be limited, forgotten, and seemingly lost to history.[29] Little has been published or easily available on-line. History is often lost when a new religious or secular body purchases an older building, and the new owner may not have access to the records or history of the previous congregation.

Sometimes the building may have remained empty and fell into disrepair or was razed as has been the experience of many beautiful Protestant congregation buildings in this community that were within a few blocks from the First Baptist Church of South Chicago. As a result, conducting research on such history is very challenging.

I remember seeing and entering many of these houses of worship[30] during the decades when I lived in South Chicago. Pictures of many of these are found in *Chicago's Southeast Side Cultural Institutions: A Community of Churches.* These were generally constructed of brick and stone or entirely of shiplap wood exteriors throughout.

Many nearby Protestant congregations were founded and built in the 1800s. These include Swedish Methodist Church/United Church of South Chicago, razed; Swedish Bethany Lutheran Church, razed. Zion Lutheran Church became Pilgrim Baptist Church an African American congregation 1929 and is extant today. This site was used in Chicago-born John D. Landis' 1980s film, *The Blues Brothers.* It has undergone extensive remodeling several times in the past and continues to serve God and the community in 2023. The only Jewish house of prayer, Agudath Achim Bikur Cholim Synagogue in South Chicago is extant but has a different congregation today. I will discuss this building later in this book.

The Spanish-speaking Baptist congregation changed its name several times over the years. It was originally named, *Primera Iglesia Bautista Mexicana, El Salvador de Sur Chicago* (First Mexican Baptist Church, The Savior, of South Chicago).

In 1933, we read in various historical references that the officials and the congregation changed its name to: *Primera Iglesia Bautista Mexicana Del Salvador De Sur Chicago,* (First Mexican Baptist Church of The Salvador of South Chicago). We note that the designation, "First," and "South Chicago" were dropped; and "*El*" became, "*Del*." This name lasted some two decades before another name changed occurred.

I have examined and found some changes about this congregation in printed sources which I have acquired over the years. These include programs between 1957-1991, membership directories published by the staff and two which I published. I find that after the fortieth anniversary in late 1966, and one celebrated in November 1970, a new name of the congregation is found on the service program. The words, "*Primera,*" "*Mexicana,*" and "*De Sur Chicago,*" were eliminated. Their new name is *Iglesia Bautista Del Salvador* (Baptist Church of The Savior).

I have read in a note from one of the congregants that this name change was the result of a misunderstanding between a Chicago City official at City Hall and the church officers who travelled there to discuss the purchase of additional land parcels which were being considered at that time.

In a way, this anomaly in name was to benefit the work of the congregation as it continued to receive new members from a variety of other Latin American countries beyond México. *Iglesia Bautista Del Salvador* is the name I have used throughout this document and may occasionally use the earlier names for clarity purposes.

Several other local congregations went through eliminating their ethnicities from their original names, e.g., German, Swedish, Scottish, or Mexican. If we had each congregation's business meeting minutes, By Laws, or service programs, I am sure we would find interesting details about when and why the changes were made, including the positive results of these changes. Nonetheless, the birth of this Spanish-speaking micro-mission to a full congregation by their founders was an act of faith in God, Christ, their deacons, congregants, and the Baptist movement in South Chicago in the 1920s.

In the early twentieth century, when the Mexican immigrants arrived in South Chicago, they were Roman Catholics, from México where they were suffering national internal turmoil and came here to survive. Those who came were not only mere immigrants. Little did they realize that in future years, they were going to be formidable assets to their adopted community, city and country.

The new arrivals also included Protestants from Texas and Midwestern states who had been introduced to the Gospel through early Baptist missionaries there. They found it was a challenge to associate with either Roman Catholics or Baptist congregations that would welcome them to worship God in South Chicago. In spite of these unfulfilled and sometimes stressful experiences, they have remained here for decades and made significant contributions.

Historical References

The Spanish-speaking Baptist believers came to South Chicago hoping to find a place where they could celebrate their faith meetings beyond those being held in their private homes. Various references provide us with information about their efforts.

In its fifty-third anniversary celebration (1926-1979), the program indicated that Rev. Moisés G. López was the pastor. He will always be remembered for his active leadership here for many years.

This event was held on Sunday, November 25, 1979, at 3:00 p.m. which was attended by members and friends of the congregation. We gathered to remember the founding of *Iglesia Bautista Del Salvador*, at 9001 S. Houston Avenue, Chicago. The anniversary preacher was Rev. Pilar Muñoz, a faithful long-time member and former full-and-part-time pastor of this congregation. The program offers a brief written history of its journey, including an historic picture taken on June 6, 1926, in front of the building, a few months before the congregation incorporated. This was twenty-four years before the Mexican congregation purchased it from the First Baptist Church of South Chicago, in 1953.

An insert in the above program titled, "*Reseñas Históricas (Historical Review)*." It succinctly captures the birth and development of this congregation. It is written in Spanish and states that during the summer of 1923, a group of Mexicans arrived in South Chicago from Texas. They soon contacted Rev. Cotton, the Pastor at the First Baptist Church of South Chicago. They requested the use of the facility for conducting services in Spanish on Sunday afternoons after English services were ended and on various weekday evenings.

This request was approved by the congregation and they began to meet. However, an issue within the nascent group arose over "who should be named the Mexican pastor." In effect, two "preachers"[31] established separate ministries in the district." This anecdote is not referenced in other information that would support this issue.

A translation of a story in *Reseñas His*tóricas, states that toward the end of 1925, seventeen Mexican immigrants from Texas arrived in South Chicago in search of employment and that they were members of the Baptist work there. It is not clear whether this is the same group that arrived in 1923, nor whether they contacted Rev. Cotton or another pastor. Nor does this second source speak to any dissent that may have occurred in its leadership.

Neither source indicates whether these Mexicans arrived here in caravans, as individuals or families, or whether they previously knew one another. Nor does it provide information about the anecdote concerning the leadership of the nascent Spanish-speaking Baptist ministry.

Having arrived here, they maintained their faith by holding worship services to God and celebrated Sunday School in their private homes or rented other venues. Somehow, various local Protestant church leaders became aware of their efforts and wished to help them by offering use of their facilities, such as Baptist pastor Rev. Cotton did in 1923.

Their presence was known by the American Baptist Home Mission Society, which was very active in Chicago and other regions for many years in outreach and support activities.

Without providing a date, the fifty-third anniversary program also tells us that the Swedish Methodist Church of South Chicago was the first Protestant congregation that offered the use of its beautiful brick and stone structure. It was located on the corner of 91st Street and S. Exchange Avenue, across the street from the South Chicago Masonic Temple and diagonally across the street from the former Saints Peter and Paul Catholic Church and school.

I remember entering the beautiful Swedish Methodist house of worship on several occasions. I saw the building undergo various exterior modifications until it was razed sometime in the 1960s-1970s or thereafter. Until I read *Reseñas Históricas* and the above reference, I was unaware that Mexican Baptist brethren sought the Methodist Swedish congregation's help.

They probably met in the pastor's office of this building. It was built in 1882, three years before the First Baptist Church of South Chicago was dedicated to God. Apparently, the conversation with the Swedish Methodist congregation did not develop into a permanent liaison in future years. Today this building no longer exists.

In *Reseñas Históricas*, we learn that two Baptist organizations also assisted the Mexican Baptist leaders to establish their congregation. One was the South Chicago Neighborhood House located at 8458 S. Mackinaw Avenue. It was six blocks north and five streets east of the First Baptist Church of South Chicago, in the *Bush* community. This American Baptist Convention-sponsored settlement house had a presence in this community since 1914. Another reference says it was part of the mission work of Hyde Park Baptist Church, an affluent congregation just north of South Chicago.

For decades, the *House*, as it was affectionately known, was an uplifting center with a myriad of programs for the nearby residents. I am very familiar with this organization and its services because, I, like thousands of children of immigrant parents from Mexico, Poland, and Ireland, were the first-generation sons and daughters who spent hours year-round in this vibrant community center.

The children who registered at the *House* were taught positive socialization development skills. We were offered sports activities for all genders. Well-educated Baptist-trained staff and volunteers led in secular and religious programs and activities based on the expected goals, objectives and funding sources. They helped us expand our learning experiences through field trips to nearby public venues, arts and crafts, camping, sports, movies and performing arts activities.

As I recall, no religious faith or doctrine was imposed on the participants. However, those who wished to engage in a such activities could do so here on Sunday morning. For many years when I was active here, the House was managed under the leadership of Rev. Basil Williams who was actively involved in many activities in the *Bush* for decades.

Reseñas Históricas states that in time, two youth leaders of the Spanish-speaking group, Francisco Villagrana and José Soledad, met with the pastor at the First Baptist Church of South Chicago, Rev. Edgar Woolhouse. They discussed how they could partner with the Baptist efforts to reach the Mexican families in the area. Four Spanish-speaking pastors assisted to establish this mission.

Early pastors were Rev. Félix T. Galindo, Rev. Carlos M. Gurrola, Rev. Florencio Santiago, and Rev. Miqueas Godínez. On October 13, 1926, under the leadership of Rev. Víctor García, the *Primera Iglesia Bautista Mexicana El Salvador de Sur Chicago,* its original name, was founded here. That was ninety-seven years ago in 2023. I cannot confirm[32] where these four pastors were ordained as Baptist ministers. They may have graduated from Spanish American Baptist Seminary in Los Angeles, which was founded in 1921, and was active in preparing Spanish-speaking Baptist pastors. Or came from a

Spanish-speaking congregation in Texas or another state before they arrived in Chicago.

They were prepared to spread the Gospel to the growing Spanish-speaking Baptist missions in California, Chicago, and across other regions of the country. I refer to Rev. Gurrola and his work in South Chicago and elsewhere in his life-long Baptist ministry. Rev. Santiago's work also continued throughout the 20th century in various Baptist Spanish-speaking congregations as in New York. I am sure the others also continued their Baptist ministry beyond their work in South Chicago for the rest of their lives.

This congregation had twenty-three active members when it began. The first Board of Directors were, brother Carlos Villagrana, Superintendent of Sunday School and General Secretary, and Rev. Víctor García their first pastor. Nine other members are listed as members of the church board. It was hosted in the building of the First Baptist Church of South Chicago.

When this significant event occurred, the receiving church members welcomed the new Mexican Baptist fellowship into their reality and both groups established a cooperative relationships in the use of the building. I recall some old time Spanish-speaking worshippers shared stories with me about how their services were originally celebrated in the basement for some years before they purchased it in 1953. When I first started attending here in the Mid-1950s, the Mexican congregants had full use of the premises.

The above two references provide two important milestones for this congregation. First, it indicates the name of the congregation was changed to, *Iglesia Bautista Mexicana Del Salvador*, in April 1933 as mentioned. It also helped us compile a list of the twenty pastors who led this congregation during fifty-three-years of Spanish-speaking Baptist service between 1926–1979. This roster[33] provides us their names, birth and death date, if known, but not the years when they served here.

Pastors of The Iglesia Bautista Del Salvador
1926-1991[34]

Rev. Víctor García
Rev. Carlos M. Gurrola (1898-1988)
Rev. Armando M. Alvarado
Rev. Raúl Echevarría
Rev. Rafael Bratton
Rev. Miqueas D. Godínez
Rev. Reinaldo Oliveres
Rev. Pilar Muñoz (1908-1994)
Rev. Efraín Balderas (1902-1987)
Rev. Tomás Montemayor (1905-1976)

Rev. Juan Junco González
Rev. Pedro Cruz
Rev. Eugenio Hanchuk
Rev. Humberto Salinas (1928-2015)
Rev. Domingo Ozuna (1943-)
Rev. Pedro B. Durik
Rev. Moisés G. López (1934-2017)
Brother Carlos Jiménez
Rev. Jacinto Muñoz Becerra (1961-)
Rev. Jeff E. Short

The congregation's sixty-second anniversary was held November 12, 1988, in this sanctuary. The program indicates that Jeff E. Short, was going to be ordained and simultaneously appointed as the congregation's new pastor. Three years later, an updated history of this congregation's sixty-fifth anniversary *Iglesia Bautista Del Salvador, 1926-1991,* was written and shared by Amelia Balderas at the service on October 27, 1991, to honor this milestone which I attended. She lists the names of pastor Short, and two other former pastors.

Of the former twenty pastors who are recorded above, only one is confirmed living at the time of this writing in 2023-2024. He is, pastor Domingo Ozuna, who served here, 1974-1975. After leaving, he returned to his home state, Texas, along with his wife, Dolores. After a while, he accepted several positions in local Baptist congregations and served as chaplain in the Dallas police department. He retired a third time in 2018, after over fifty-years of Baptist ministry. However, a bilingual congregation *Iglesia Bautista El Calvario* needed a pastor and eagerly sought brother Domingo to lead them. He accepted and continues to serve God and the community here in 2022. He states that he once preached in this congregation when he was about ten years old.

Another former pastor Rev. Short, may still be living but I have not confirmed this after trying to reach him. I understand he earned a Doctorate probably after leaving this congregation or was earning it while he pastored in South Chicago. If alive, he probably serves in a large congregation wherever he lives.

Our pastors were all married, strived to be good Christian husbands, and fathers to from two to five children. Most of the pastors tenures here were brief as full-time, part-time, or as ad hoc. Several recycled to the pulpit over the years.

Three such Pastors were Rev. Ralph Bratton, Rev. Cesar O. Mascareñas (1924-2019), who died in California, and Rev. Marvin Berry. I recall that Rev. Mascareñas studied for years to be a nurse, though I cannot confirm whether he was employed in this medical profession. Rev. Balderas and Rev. Muñoz recycled many times over the years.

Our ad hoc pastors would arrive in the building early in the morning from wherever they lived. They would preach and participate in the full service. Often, they were scheduled to bring the Sunday evening message as well. In between services, they were hosted by members of the congregation in order to be in the pulpit for the second service.

A few of our regular pastors had secular employment in the nearby steel mills while they faithfully served in Sunday morning and evening in addition to ministering the Wednesday evenings services or other special programs. Pastors Muñoz, Balderas, Montemayor, and López worked in the steel mills in South Chicago or nearby Indiana Harbor area industries.

The pastors had office hours on a limited basis in the small office space behind the baptistry. Most worked out of their homes without staff, volunteers, or modern electronic technology that is available to all pastors today.

Nonetheless, each was ready to minister as scheduled or during emergencies or unexpected special needs by the congregants. They were sometimes absent from the pulpit due to their personal work schedules and ad hoc pastors were invited to assist. I served closely with a few of these pastors by providing piano or organ music in services here and accompanied them in other venues.

Each pastor dedicated many years of service to Christ; a few were new to being part-or-full-time pastors at other congregations; some had previously attended and graduated from Baptist seminary or Bible Institute studies associated with colleges in other states, or in Latin American countries.

The pastors prepared themselves for the ministry through years of personal studies in the Word and proved themselves spiritually and gained ministerial experience enough to be ordained through the oversight of a Baptist congregation where they studied or worked.

This was the case for brother López, and brother Short. Brother López was ordained here as pastor and minister in a beautiful "*Servicio de Ordenación*" (Ordination Service), on Sunday morning, November 27, 1977. A host of visiting and former pastors, friends, family, members of this congregation, and I participated in this event.

One of our in-house poets for many years, Pedro A. Ruíz, wrote, recited, and dedicated a moving and beautiful twenty-stanza poem about brother López. The poem described and compared him to a valiant and faithful warrior for Christ. A special dedicatory duet was sung by Frank and Elisa Dávila Pérez, long-time members of this congregation. Rev. Pilar Muñoz delivered words of Christian counsel to the new pastor to consider as he began his pastoral work. Rev. Marvin Berry, a former ad hoc pastor here shared Christian counsel to the congregation. Congregation Deacon, Antonio Pérez, presented the newly ordained minister to the audience. Brother López served Christ here before and after his ordination for years. Frank left us in late November 2023 at ninety-two years of age.

I recall the pastors had interesting personalities. Each knew the Bible scriptures extensively and homiletics emphatically in order to prepare and deliver their messages. I considered several of these pastors as wise apologists for preaching the Gospel of Christ. They were happy and good men. They loved to sing Christian hymns and some dared to compose melodies of their own.

Pastor Muñoz and I were to meet and write the music for his rendition of the moving nine-verse Psalm 47: "O Clap your hands, all ye people shout unto God with the voice of triumph." Our schedules did not permit us time to complete this effort, but I can still play most of the beautiful melody he developed. He certainly loved to bring the Word, write poetry and sing.

When he was not preaching, Pastor Salinas enjoyed playing his Mexican marimba brought here from his birthplace, Mérida, Yucatán, México, since the first day he arrived in South Chicago. Pastor Durik was a word smither who loved to share his insightful and moving poetry related to Christian themes. These were often inserted into the Sunday service programs. He wrote a beautiful piece for the Christmas Program in 1976. It poignantly expresses the Good News about the Nativity and the arrival of Christ the Savior to the world.

Some of our pastors were bespectacled. I can remember them as they stood behind the beautiful and attractive large wood lectern on the pulpit. Often when speaking, they would look over the rims of their glasses and ask a question to the general audience or a specific person about what he was expounding. I recall that this look seemed to put some people in suspense thinking the question might be directed to them. This happened to me several times.

Our pastors were *aficionados* of our Latino secular and Christian history. They enjoyed sharing interesting conversations. They spoke with anyone on subjects of the day or having historical meaning to our community or about the Bible. Each was ebullient, bilingual, and bicultural in English and Spanish, and tireless men.

Because our pastors studied the Word in Spanish and lived in community where Cervantes' language was generally used in our services or daily conversations, our vocabulary was enriched with new or infrequently words. These enhanced our understanding of the message being preached as well as in dialogs with them.

We had a few Anglo ministers who served here. These were Rev. Bratton, Rev. Berry, Rev. Hanchuk, Rev. Durik, and Pastor Short. Each was fully competent in Spanish and English and adept in the Mexican culture. Reverends Bratton, Berry and Short were American born. Rev. Eugenio Hanchuk was Romanian born who lived in Latin America for many years before he arrived in South Chicago. I do not recall in which European country Rev. Durik country was born or lived in Latin America. I remember each of these pastors were caring ministers and fully embraced by the congregation.

I personally served with eleven pastors of the above thirteen beginning with Rev. Muñoz. It was a joy serving with each of them. I do not recall Rev. Jimenez' and I only met Rev. Short at the closing service here in 1991.

PART III:
MEXICANS PURCHASE THE BAPTIST BUILDING (1953)

Description of Building and Neighborhood

I often wondered if the Mexican leaders of *Iglesia Bautista Del Salvador* had any knowledge or history about the building they bought in 1953.[35] To them, I am sure, it was a beautiful dream come true after having started their Christian journey in the Baptist tradition some twenty-seven years earlier as a Spanish-speaking Baptist Mission within the First Baptist Church of South Chicago.

I recall stories that many congregants believed this purchase was a gift from God to encourage them to proceed with spreading the Gospel to the Spanish-speaking community. They felt a certain level of Christian "satisfación y humildad (satisfaction and humility)," they had progressed to this level.

This decision would enhance and strengthen this church for years to come. Their action must have brought them congratulations from their Baptist colleagues on having achieved this milestone. A review of what they did and their historical and spiritual trajectory with the First Baptist Church of South Chicago follows.

The large wood-frame one-story building at 9001 and S. Houston Avenue was constructed by the congregation of the First Baptist Church of South Chicago in 1885 as I learned in 2020. However, as stated earlier above, the congregation may have possibly had an earlier structure and was seeking aid from other Baptist churches to complete "...a needed addition[36] to their church edifice," as stated in *Inter Ocean Newspaper* on February 22, 1885.

I have referenced this article earlier in this document in trying to understand what the "addition" implied. The only structure I have confirmed continues to exist at this site with few people alive today who are aware of its original design. It was built years before many of other houses of worship, private residences, multi-unit apartments, and commercial buildings were constructed in and around S. Houston Avenue.

The members of the First Baptist Church of South Chicago constructed this building on the natural swampy black soil and sandy terrain found throughout most of South Chicago and other nearby communities that existed then and is extant today. In my youth I remember that a particular two-storied wood-framed building along East 91st Street and S. Buffalo Avenue, just one block south and east of the First Baptist Church building was tilting in an easterly direction in a very dangerous condition. There was also another small wood-framed residence on the corner of 90th and S. Muskegon Avenue near Bessemer Park that was tilting in a serious degree off-center to the south. I could not understand how these buildings remained standing for years in such conditions. By the time I was a sophomore in Bowen High School in 1955, both of these buildings were demolished by the city or owners before they toppled over.

The soil where the First Baptist Church of South Chicago decided to construct was fortunately a reliable location compared to the condition of the two residences mentioned above. The building is extant in 2024 after 139-years of Christian service. I am convinced that it was originally built some eight feet below the sidewalk level which we see today. I surmise that between 1885 and 1890, it was raised a few feet voluntarily to conform with the new street level imposed by City of Chicago for health and sanitation concerns. This is when the cement blocks were used on the basement walls. Other suggested changes to the structure are discussed below.

In order to glean information about the building's construction date and design, I reviewed the 1897 Sanborn Fire Insurance Map[37] from Chicago, Cook County, Illinois. The map Image Number 40 shows this reference. It provides information about the general size of the parcel owned by the congregation and other adjacent ones. It indicates there are five parcels within a larger parcel which starts at 90th Street on the east side of S. Houston Avenue. As I surmised, it indicates the entrance to the building was near the corner of 252 E.

90th Street, its original address, and faced north as seen in the photograph I researched.

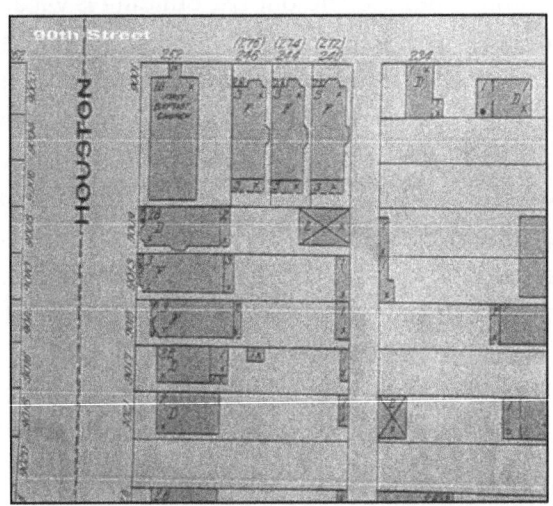

Sanborn Fire Insurance Map, 1897, Source: Library of Congress.

The top of the above map image reveals the front elevations of five parcels including the Baptist's larger one at the left top of the drawing. Its protruding original entrance with the "IX" faces north at the intersections of S. Houston Avenue and 90th Street (east). The address is 252. The words "First Baptist Church" are found on the darkened roof of the building's image. The lighter shaded parcel to the right (east), was probably owned by the First Baptist Church of South Chicago since it was built in 1885. This one parcel and the building were purchased by *Iglesia Bautista Del Salvador* in 1953.

The three long darker shaded parcels at the top of the image and to the right with the lower addresses 246, 244, and 240, are the parcels that will be subsequently purchased by Iglesia Bautista Del Salvador in 1965.

It is unclear why the other three different numbers are shown above the aforesaid numbers. The lowest address starts in the east with subsequent addresses increasing in a westerly direction. In contemporary Chicago, the lowest street numbers start from the west and increase as they move east, with avenue designations shown as north to south.

One parcel image next to the Baptist building is vacant without an image structure or address. However, from the undated historic photo I acquired in early March 2020 of the building, we are partially able to see the roof and wooden siding of a building immediately adjacent to the east edge of the Baptist building. This could be the vacant parcel of a house that did not exist in the image of the 1897 Sanborn map. This and the other three parcels became crucial factors in the purchase price and tax issues when *Iglesia Bautista Del Salvador* attempted to them buy during the exciting growth history of this congregation during 1950-1960s.

Perhaps some clarification of the numbering can be explained if we consider that in 1908-1909 the City of Chicago passed an ordinance to improve the residential renumbering system. The system facilitated finding an address outside of the Chicago Loop area. It was amended again later. This may explain why the numbering system is different today than in earlier years. Since then, these previous former three-digit addresses would be in 3200 East Street 90th and S. Houston Avenue.

William Martin's study *Chicago Street Changes*[38] explains why a consistent numbering system for residents' homes was seriously needed. It compiled in alphabetical order the history of the street names from earliest times to the most current. His study does not provide dates about when these were implemented.

Houston Avenue had at least six previous names in this order: Graham Street, Parnell Avenue, Reade Avenue, Reade Street, Cedar Street, and Stephens Street. Five of these seem to have been derived from surnames and one from the study of botany. Of course, the ultimate name, Houston Avenue had to be to honor Gen. Sam Houston (1793-1863), Texas President before this Southwest territory entered the Union in 1836 and re-elected in 1841.

I could not ascertain why and when City Officials decided to name this Avenue to honor Gen. Houston. However, his many achievements were considered more heavily than other historic or contemporary names when South Chicago street names were being assigned. A few other familiar dignitaries more closely linked to Chicago's and South Chicago's history did have their names celebrated on other local avenues and public buildings.

A few examples are, August Harris Burley (organized Chicago's first fire department), Daniel Burnham (public park beautification and infrastructure), Schuler Colfax (Illinois Central Railroad Vice President, and a U.S. Vice President), Gen. Philip Henry Sheridan (U.S. Civil War, and Commander in Chicago Fire protector in 1871), Colonel James Harvey Bowen (sobriquet "Father of South Chicago," and industrialist), and John N. Thorp (early steel industrialist in South Chicago). Each of these men were significant leaders and most probably walked the streets of South Chicago and helped in the development of the City of Chicago during 1800s-1900s.

After local streets were raised in certain parts of South Chicago, in time, dirt streets and wooden walkways were generally paved with concrete. Some streets were laid with small rectangular brown cobblestone bricks such as I saw in many European country streets. These were manually laid on streets and alleyways throughout South Chicago. I walked and drove on them on S. Houston Avenue in front of the Baptist building and several blocks north and south on this street. They were readily observable for decades before they were paved over with asphalt in 1950-1960.

In 2023, cobble stone brick streets still exist. They may be seen in the alleyway where the second South Chicago Elementary School (1876) and the original Bowen High School began (1882) near 93rd Street and S. Houston Avenue stood. They are also found in the alleyway entrance along E. 89th Street near the former Green Bay Avenue the entrance to the former U.S. Steel Company close to where I lived for some eight years.

Wide concrete raised sidewalks were poured by the City of Chicago around the Baptist building on the S. Houston Avenue and 90th Street and are not seen in the early photo of this intersection.

Other streets throughout greater South Chicago and East Side communities saw similar drastically needed infrastructural changes.

From the undated photo I received in early 2021, we see that when the building was constructed, there was a doorway near the corner of the northwest wall of the building. When people exited the sanctuary, they passed through the doorway, into a small entryway, and onto a stairway to exit as they faced west onto 3200 S. Houston Avenue, or the actual current address of 9001 S. Houston Avenue. The Sanborn Map does not reveal whether the building was on the natural ground elevation or raised.

The photo reveals several peculiarities about the sidewalks that surround it. The wooden sidewalks on S. Houston Avenue and 90th Street do not touch the building leaving a void of some six feet between them. The basement's six windows and one door are seen on S. Houston Avenue with a basement window on 90th Street as the wood planked sidewalk descend slightly toward the then existing building next door to the east.

Wood posts and cross planks are seen around the original building which served as safety barriers to protect the passersby from falling into the void between the top of the sidewalk to the ground below. The streets are unpaved sans curbs, lights, stop signs, or fire hydrants. Complete public infrastructure had not arrived in parts of South Chicago until sporadically seen in later years.

In addition to information above about the building, we see its architectural design is executed in very simple straight lines. It lacks a simple cornerstone as is found on the Emmanuel Lutheran Church (1907) to the south or imbedded in the former Jewish temple (1902) to the north.

The original Baptist building had a simple medium sized wooden tower which jutted out of the north corner of the roof on S. Houston Avenue. It was some fifteen feet tall. It may have served as a campanile and was removed when the building was raised and extended. It was not a quasi-stand-alone multi-floored tower as was the one of nearby First Congregational Church of South Chicago, also known as Bird Memorial Center. Nor was it as tall as any of the steeples which could be seen and are extant on several other immigrant founded church buildings in South Chicago today.

I was unable to ascertain when the building was raised nor how many times. When the concrete sidewalks were poured, this literally enclosed the exterior perimeter around the building and closed the void between it on S. Houston Avenue.

Two sprawling elm trees on the corner of 90th Street and S. Houston Avenue were planted decades before the 1950s. Their foliage and broad branches still provide pleasant shade for the passersby's and congregants as they exit the building during local hot and sunny days. Recently, the City of Chicago implemented the *Streetscape Design Guidelines* with community leaders to improve streetscapes on S. Houston Avenue and other neighborhood streets.

As a result, various beautification projects were undertaken in 2003 to improve traffic flow and the beautification of neighborhood streets in order to make them pedestrian friendly. The results of these efforts are seen in nearby Hegewisch community's business district streets. The engineering design needed to implement and complete the arboreal project was quite a fete. On S. Houston and Commercial Avenues, planters were used, or holes were cut through the raised vaulted sidewalks. Concrete encasements were poured underneath the holes to enhance the root system for the variety of young trees that were planted in them and continue to grow in 2024.

Prior to the tree project, the sidewalks in these two and other South Chicago neighborhood streets were solid concrete except for the round holes and iron covers located in front of the homes or businesses. These were mainly used for coal drops. Natural beauty has been returned through these projects to beautify the working-class neighborhood.

The building's dimensions for the former Baptist Church are stated in Coldwell Banker Residential Broker sales announcement[39] in 2019. The width is 75-feet by 120-feet-long. Other information indicates there are 3,131-square-feet on the first floor and 3,000 square feet in a finished walkout basement. These dimensions were fully reached when the building was expanded from its original smaller size.

During the 1970s, the Spanish-speaking Baptist owners enclosed the entire parcel with a steel six-foot wire hurricane fence to keep the weed and grass-covered property from being used as illegal garbage or other unauthorized purpose site. During 2019-2022 changes have been made by the current owners, *Iglesia La Luz Del Mundo* (The Light Of The World Church) and are discussed below.

The former Baptist building has always appeared unusual on S. Houston Avenue. Its exterior walls run south and north rather than from east to west as do nearly all the buildings on this and many streets throughout South Chicago.

In March 2020, my plans to travel from California to Chicago to research information about the Baptist Church building history and its leadership were curtailed by the unexpected arrival in the U.S. of the COVID-19 pandemic.

My alternative was to continue reviewing documents which I had accumulated serendipitously over the years sans a thought of writing a history about this congregation. I asked several of my friends if they had any historic materials which they might lend me to use in my work. I also acquired information on-line that was useful in finding documents and articles. I also learned there were documents that are only available at various venues such as universities, local history centers, and private and public libraries. I was determined to move forward with writing this book by using all possible sources.

In October 2020, I learned from a review[40] of the Chicago Data Portal of 2015, that approximately seven of the extant residential buildings on the east side of S. Houston Avenue where the Baptist building is located were built in the 1800s. Their construction dates are: 1878, 1883, 1888 (two), 1893, 1894, and 1898, and are mostly made of wood. I believe other local residential and commercial streets have one or two buildings slightly older or as old as these. They are in danger as developers see an opportunity to buy the land or buildings.

Facilitator in Establishing the First Mexican Baptist Church in South Chicago

Across the street on the west side of the former Baptist building are ten structures built between 1868-1898. They are residential homes built of wood, brick, or a combination of both materials, in various architectural designs and sizes and remain extant. The house at 9002 S. Houston Avenue has the earliest date although it does not appear to be as old as referenced in the above source. It's basement was used in one of the scenes of *The Fugitive* movie. Most buildings are multiple-family two-story residences. One is a large brick two-lot multi-family structure used for rental of apartments. There are no bungalows on this street. The west side of 90th and S. Houston Avenue has experienced no real demolition compared to the east side where the Baptist building is located.

An on-line review in September 2020 and an on-site visit in 2022 reveal that some century-old-structures have been demolished on the side of S. Houston Avenue where the old Baptist building stands. Today, one can clearly see empty lots and the eight-feet elevation difference between the surface of the sidewalk to the natural elevation below. This terrain has been hidden from the public for over one hundred years.

Since the mills closed, nearby streets and intersections of this part of South Chicago are skeletons of what they were. From the 1880s until the late 1960s, this immediate area was the very pulse of the community. About every need and service could be obtained from a family-owned business: fresh produce, fresh fish, live and dressed fowl, ethnic bread and pastry, household goods, personal and business needs, furniture, restaurants, education, clothing, banking, photography, law offices, medical services, funeral parlors, several theatrical and movie venues, saloons, hotels, hardware stores and automotive repair businesses. Most of these enterprises are gone although a renaissance is slowly taking place.

A study in 2016 reveals plans to revitalize Commercial Avenue, the main business sector of South Chicago for over one-hundred years. It may be perused in a report published by the Great Cities Institute from the University of Illinois Chicago. Several local elected and community leaders were on the committee that prepared this report. These plans are active in 2022.

The original Baptist building dimensions and the fact that wood was principally used in its construction is revealing. This created a major challenge for heating during Chicago's harsh winters and cooling the premises during the torrid and humid summer months. The congregation's income level and budget determined that wood and not brick was used in its construction. The building's massive, slanted roof gives the sanctuary a sharp apex in the center. The original structure had no interior wall insulation anywhere. When it snowed, the interior heat passed through the sanctuary's ceiling, up through the attic, and onto the roof which quickly melted the new or previously fallen snow.

Critically needed roof rain gutters and downspouts on the east and west sides of the roof were not installed in 1885 or by any of the congregations until *Iglesia La Luz Del Mundo* did so some time in 2020-2021. Historically, when it rained, it usually created a cascade of water onto the empty lot on the east and west side sidewalk area with seepage into the basement from both sources. During the winter months, two foot-long, saber-and-dagger like icicles formed on the edges of the roof and fell onto the sidewalk below creating a treacherous path for any passersby.

Lighting in the sanctuary was minimal. I recall the interior ceiling of the sanctuary had four archaic light fixtures which were suspended by iron link chains, not the polished brass usually found in sanctuary light accoutrements. Large incandescent bulbs were placed inside white opaque glass covers shaped like inverted pyramids. The fixtures were probably not the original gas burning from 1885. These were probably installed after 1909 when electricity arrived in Chicago for general public usage states Harold Platt on this topic. When I first saw the interior of this room in the mid-1950s, I was probably looking at a second-generation lighting system that went from gas light to incandescent lighting which was already several decades old. One day as I looked up at the sanctuary ceiling in the late 1950s, I saw old lead gas pipes that had been capped in the past but not removed. They were protruding slightly next to the electric fixtures. I was convinced these supplied natural gas to the light fixtures to illuminate this room, attic area, basement and stairways when the Baptist building was built. This last system was improved by *La Iglesia La Luz Del Mundo* in 2021-2022 when they extensively modernized the interior of the sanctuary along with the entire electrical system in the building.

One snowy evening in the 1960s while standing in the north entrance vestibule waiting for a group of youth to arrive I recognized an old gas light brass fixture that was attached to the north wall of this room. It was covered by a dark red round globe with a small valve on its brass stem. I turned it and smelled the natural gas fumes coming from the fixture's spigot. I recognized the fixture as the kind used in the building's early fire escape exit system. This was removed later.

During the mid-1950s, the building's interior genuine plaster walls were painted light beige while leaving the wood trim with a dark walnut color. This color was susceptible to showing soot marks on the walls, especially over the area over the radiators. During 1960s-1970s, the interior of the building was painted a "battleship gray" as was expressed in soto voce by some parishioners who did not like this color.

A few years later, the men received permission to paint the walls in the building again. They chose a lite blue color while the wood trim remained dark brown. The wall soot issue was persistent and perennial no matter what color was used.

The south wall of this room occasionally had a phrase placed on it as, "*Bienvenidos (*Welcome)," or another Biblical phrases in beautiful lettering. There were never any arched carved oak beams overhead spanning the sanctuary with cherubim looking down upon the congregants as found in some church sanctuaries. The walls were plain, with no niches to hold statues or other accoutrements. The pews were made of sturdy brown oak wood which complemented the ecclesiastical design of the long, beautiful lancet-design windows.

The 1885 *Chicago Tribune* article referenced above describes the "Church Dedication" which took place at that time. It said the new sanctuary was made beautiful for this historic service. It does not provide information about windows. In the only photo we have of the original building we see lancet-styled windows everywhere but cannot confirm whether they were stained or regular plain glass.

If we assume the original windows were made of stained glass and were the ones I saw when I worshipped here, they were simple yet beautiful in their overall design and none used double glass. They lacked tracery or ribbing seen in mighty church buildings throughout Chicago and in other local Protestant and Catholic houses of prayer. The glass panels used simple lead caulking to maintain their integrity.

The original building had five lancet-shaped windows on the west wall. The east wall had five lancet-shaped windows with the design described above but one of them was a shorter twin-window near the northeast side of the wall. Raising and lowering of each window was facilitated by a mechanism that used two medium sized heavy torpedo-shaped iron weights attached to ropes within the side recesses.

The stained glass windowpanes were delicately cut in rectangular pieces in hews of tan, green, and brown with smaller rectangles around the curved or straight edge of the wood frame. The panes were joined to each other and connected to the wood frame by the lead caulking. The windows brought beautiful soft gold and tan colored streams of tan light into the sanctuary throughout the day. At night when the lights were on in the sanctuary, passersby outside enjoyed the beauty of the stained-glass colors shining through them. Sadly, missing and broken panes often affected indoor temperatures and replacements with plain glass diminished the overall beauty of the windows.

Several of the windows had brief memorial notations embedded in the rectangular glass panels at the bottom of each. The name of the family or person who contributed the window was inscribed in the glass, with some having dates of dedication. A full history of the

Facilitator in Establishing the First Mexican Baptist Church in South Chicago

windows might inform us as to when these were originally installed and some information about the family or person being memorialized in each.

When I moved from South Chicago to Normal, Illinois to complete my undergraduate and begin graduate university studies (1967-1970), two major building projects were launched. These were to replace the sanctuary windows described above and cover the interior sanctuary walls with dark brown wood panels. While these were major structural changes and enigmatic for some parishioners, it did not affect the church's overall mission to preach the Gospel.

During a visit to Chicago in August 2021, and again in June 2022, I saw that *Iglesia La Luz Del Mundo* had reduced the four windows on the east and west walls to three on each side. The interior of each was covered with adjustable blue curtains. I could not determine whether plain or frosted glass was used but they were smaller than the ones that *Iglesia Bautista Del Salvador* had replaced in previous years.

First Baptist Church of South Chicago has been surrounded by several historic Christian churches and one Jewish congregation. All were within walking distance of this church. Each was founded by Roman Catholic, German, Swedish, Polish, Irish, Jewish or other European immigrants to serve their particular ethnic group. Today, the extant buildings of these congregations are over a century old and are struggling to survive or are closed due to economic and social factors experienced in South Chicago. Of those that are extant, we see remnants of their early structures. I recall some of the family members they served and the activities they celebrated. In my youthful years, I lived and played with some of the children who were members of several of these houses of worship.

A few yards south at 9031 S. Houston Avenue, we find the second building of the former Immanuel Lutheran Church (1908). James Huenink states that in the early 1870s James Harvey Bowen, President of The Calumet & Chicago Canal & Company, donated three lots to the fledgling congregation. After reaching its one-hundredth anniversary in 1973 of serving Christ and its German and Swedish communicants, it closed its doors. Its second elementary school was built during the twentieth century and was closed then razed either before or after the congregation closed. I remember seeing children in this school. I often thought how exciting it was to be enrolled in the small school next to their church.

Since it closed, this house of worship has been used intermittently by various religious groups in need of a house of worship. In 2024, the building is extant as is its magnificent over 150 feet tall green copper steeple and cross though the bells within the steeple have been silent for many decades. In 2023, behind the majestic brick church building, I saw a small wooden house in serious need of repair. This century old wooden house was probably where the pastors and their families lived.

Similarly, a more than a century-old multi-colored brick building north of the Lutheran church and the former Baptist congregation on S. Houston Avenue, is another historic building. It is the former Jewish Orthodox Agudath Achim Bikur Cholim Synagogue, built in 1902. In 1972 after almost some ninety-five years of serving this community, it closed due to its inability to sustain a quorum of ten men needed to lead their services and low membership.

The twin octagon-shaped towers still exist sans a prominent Star of David which crowned each of these and the center of the roof's front. The façade remains intact. Its entrance is crowned with three half-circle arches uniquely embedded with Hebrew expressions which must be significant to the Jewish community, and to anyone who can interpret them. Above the entrance are five small medium arched stained-glass windows connected to one another. I surmise these represent the first five books of the Jewish Torah of Genesis, Exodus, Leviticus, Numbers and Deuteronomy, also known as The Pentateuch in the Christian faith.

A large octagon, stained glass window located in the upper center of the former temple's massive exterior east brick wall contains the beautiful Star of David imbedded in it. I remember seeing this building as a youth and wondered what it represented. In later years I learned about the interwoven history and how Christianity was born out of the young Jewish Jesus of Nazareth and His followers.

During one of my visits to Chicago in August 2021, I noticed the black iron gates at the entrance to the building were partially agar. I dared myself to stop my car to fulfill the long-awaited opportunity to enter the building. Nearing it, I saw a large sign posted on the front right-side wall. It listed the name of the Senior pastor Rev. Emmanuel Soji Adesanya, and other information about it being a, "Miracles & Winners Place."

I quietly entered and found a small group of some thirteen well-dressed African Black men and women parishioners seated together. They were listening to a woman speaking in English with an African or Caribbean accent. She was expounding from a text she held in her hand. She was preaching about the need for people to be careful to not let one's personal riches distract them from being aware of and helping people in need as is found in Proverbs 22, and I Timothy 6, which discuss this topic. The audience verbally approved her words.

I saw artifacts that were used by the former Jewish worshipers. There were beautiful oak pews which had wooden text holders attached to the length of the back of each. I had never seen this style of book holder in any Christian house of worship. Also, I was attracted to the beauty of three huge, three-tiered glistening crystal chandeliers hanging from gold-colored chains attached to a sixty-feet high ceiling of the square shaped sanctuary.

They were beautiful as they hung between four square wall pillars in the room. They appeared to be original fixtures, unlike the humbler ones found in *Iglesia Bautista Del Salvador*. I also noticed the small half-circle windows high above the east walls had Jewish symbols or writing on them. They were sealed but not removed and appeared to be covered so that sunlight would not shine through their stained-glass.

Other half-circle windows on the north and south walls have also been modified with brightly colored glass or plastic covers. Some had written messages in English. I saw but did not visit the balcony in back of the room. I understand that in times past, when synagogue services were held, women were required to sit here apart from the men.

I remember as a youth I saw the sanctuary which had an elevated square wooden pulpit where the rabbi stood and rocked as he lead the service. On this visit, I saw that it was gone. It was probably removed by any of the owners after the original Jewish congregation vacate the premises. I remember that on Jewish high holidays, their parishioners would double-park their cars on S. Houston Avenue and slowed traffic as it moved past the front of the synagogue.

A Spanish-speaking Pentecostal congregation on the east side of 92nd and S. Houston Avenue was founded during the 1950s. They continue to meet the spiritual and social needs of their parishioners. They have maintained their large brick building for many years. Other smaller bilingual store-front Pentecostal congregations used to be active in South Chicago for decades as well.

Interestingly, some thirty feet east of the alleyway of the historic Baptist building, for many years there existed a small wood-framed residential structure. In the annals of time, it was converted to a house of worship by a group of African American congregants. I occasionally saw people on the premises but they never appeared to participate in any activities within or outside of their premises.

This group may have owned or rented the building. Over the years, it fell into disrepair and disappeared sometime in the 1960's after being empty for many years. In 2023, the site where the house existed remains empty, and the soil has been leveled and covered with grass. I believe there is scant information available about their history in South Chicago.

In addition to the extant houses of worship, many residential structures still surround the former Baptist structure. These buildings have stood here as centurions throughout the development of this community. Each generally occupies a single, narrow parcel of land running in an east to west direction. By contrast, the Baptist building property occupies several parcels and is listed under one address, 9001 S. Houston Avenue, which runs parallel to the street, in a north

Facilitator in Establishing the First Mexican Baptist Church in South Chicago

and south direction as discussed above. This direction is rare for buildings throughout South Chicago. It abuts the first private home adjacent to the church building at 9009 S. Houston Avenue, the south terminus of the old Baptist structure. The brief information I have of this building indicates it was constructed in 1894 and is extant in 2023.

In the recent past, I researched the history as to when the street levels and buildings were raised in South Chicago. I have minimal information as to when such massive infrastructure projects occurred in this community. As happened in the northern part of early Chicago streets, poor drainage and standing polluted water brought various kinds of dysentery or other water-born issues caused by the soil flooding and retaining water for days.

To resolve similar problems in South Chicago, scientists and engineers convinced South Chicago residents, business and residential owners, and City fathers that entire buildings needed and could be raised safely. Such engineering projects were successfully undertaken in Europe and Chicago and could be accomplished here, the leaders believed.

An earlier and extraordinary example of raising buildings took place in downtown Chicago in 1861. This grandiose event[41] occurred at the corner of Lake Street and Dearborn Street when the brick four-storied Tremont House Hotel was raised six-feet above its original foundation to the new street level even while some distinguished and every-day occupants remained in the structure.

In order to do this, an up-and-coming local entrepreneurial resident of that era, George Pullman and two other members directed five-hundred men who worked in trenches beneath the building. Upon blowing a whistle at given intervals, the workers ingeniously turned five-thousand jackscrews to slowly raise the building without disturbing the occupants.

Mr. Pullman used this approach in other projects. He is the same industrialist who in just a few years into the future would partner with Col. James H. Bowen to found and develop a large bucolic and swampy Lake Calumet area into the future greater community which would include South Chicago. Col. Bowen is still remembered in historic discussions as the "Father of South Chicago" for the myriad of industrial projects he launched in this area.

In 1881, Mr. Pullman established the Village of Pullman where his employees, bosses, and their families could live comfortably within their skill and salary ranges. The entire workforce lived in brick steam-heated town houses. His company constructed a massive number of other large, long manufacturing structures and a vast campus in order to establish the Pullman sleeping car railroad industry. The entire enterprise was a sprawling town just a few miles south and west of the Baptist building. It would be interesting to know whether any residents of this church were employed by this company over the years it operated. Today, the area is a national historic monument and is being restored as a viable community sans the industrial operations.

During the mid-1800s, streets in South Chicago, and particularly most of S. Houston Avenue and others throughout the community needed to be raised as said above. Raising each building was at the owner's expense to align the first floor of the building with the new height of the street. If the owner opted out of this decision, the first floor would become the basement, as is seen in many houses on both sides of S. Houston Avenue and throughout several other streets in South Chicago. These houses would require a short walkway to enter the new first floor, and stairways were needed to get to the new basement.

Commercial Avenue which runs north and south between 87th Street and 93rd Street was raised. We find a description[42] of how this was accomplished in a newspaper article written by Arthur Pollard, "Paving of Streets Requires 12-foot Stone Wall." It reflected what he saw forty-nine years before he wrote this two-column observation while walking around South Chicago in July 1892. Pollard said he was,

> "...amazed at the amount of water that was standing on most of the vacant property, and that the paving of the streets required a twelve-foot strong wall to be erected on each side

of the street and then the filling in process would take place. A railroad track was built on the original level of Commercial Ave. and long strings of gondola cars with sand being unloaded by hand to fill in, and as filling took place the track was raised until finished from 87th street to 93rd^d Street. 92nd street had previously been raised by the same method of filling. Looking northwest from (the) corner of 87th street and Commercial Ave. there was a large body of water over territory extending to South Chicago Ave. and it was known as Lake Wirora."

The lake name is interesting, and the view must have been breathtaking. In reality, it was probably the vast numbers of acres of standing rainwater that appeared to be a lake and locally given this mystical name. I could not find information about it. This entire area quickly became wood and brick homes during the 19th-20th centuries. In 2024, many are extant, others need major repairs, and when razed, they leave empty parcels in their place.

Today, the massive engineering fete Pollard describes is extant everywhere within walking distance of the former First Baptist Church building. Looking west from the corner of 90th Street and S. Houston Avenue to Commercial Avenue, we see 90th Street slopes downward to the original grade upon reaching Exchange Avenue and continues west in this manner.

It is obvious that when the Baptist building was constructed in 1885, its basement floor was on the natural elevation. Thereafter, when the City of Chicago decided to raise the streets in this part of South Chicago to resolve the drainage and other issues, between mid-1880 to mid-1890s, it was raised. When concrete blocks replaced the original wood basement infrastructure, the building was raised again to create a higher basement and building.

The Baptist congregation had the resources and may have hired a company to do this, or they did it themselves. Other proprietors did not. Thus, even in 2024 we see variations in first-floor entrances in some buildings that are still located below the sidewalk elevation, and their second floor is their main entrance. This required adding a short concrete or wooden walkway from the raised street to the new height of the first floor of the building.

It would be interesting to have details as to the number of jackscrews used to raise the Baptist building, the start and end date of the project, and the cost incurred by this small congregation. While such a project is well documented about the famous Tremont House in downtown Chicago, similar documentation about the First Baptist Church of South Chicago is not readily found though it must exist somewhere.

We see a perfect example of this effect in the second elementary public school at 91st and S. Houston Avenue. Its first building was constructed in 1876. It was built of brick and sandstone on the original grade elevation. Starting in 1882, the attic of this school is where with Bowen high school studies began. In 1889, an extension was added. When the street level was raised, there was a variance between the first floor and the street. This required building modification which were done and seen for decades. Both buildings were razed in early summer of 1946. The land where this campus stood has been a fenced parking lot for seventy-eight years sans a public park that was discussed as a possible use of this site.

As is well known, in 1910, a new high school campus was opened at another location, and some of its academic programs and students were transferred here, leaving the older building to offer some classes and space for other community uses.

An additional impact of raising the sidewalk added height to the walls and roof of the 1885 Baptist building. This change added several more feet above the sidewalk to the bottom of the eaves of the roof. Also, any additional feet was added to the height of the top of the roof as is seen today.

The entrance of the building was changed from its original address of 252 E. 90th Street as shown in the Sanborn Map shown. The church's new address is 9001 S. Houston Avenue, a few feet west around the corner of the earlier entrance. The original ground level basement entrance seen in the center of the old photograph was moved to the south end of the building at the new sidewalk elevation.

When it was ultimately raised, amenities followed. The basement had twenty-one rectangular clear glass windows. It was expanded and finished out in later years. This probably added slightly more usable square feet to each floor in the building. The basement walls are approximately twenty to twenty-five feet high from floor to ceiling. Sometime in the 1950s and thereafter, the Baptist Spanish-speaking congregation made some modifications to various interior sections of the building, and changes were continuous over the decades.

I witnessed men covering the interior basement walls with knotty pine wood panels in the 1950s-1960s. This change brightened the ambience of this part of the House of God. This wood design was totally replaced by *Iglesia La Luz Del Mundo* by 2022 with drywall and painted white along with other changes on the floor and ceiling structural area.

The original basement floor was laid using long, solid oak planks. As years passed, whenever it rained the floor buckled as water seeped in beneath the east wall of the basement due to the leaky foundation. Also, the poorly sealed raised sidewalks had vaults under them on the west wall which also allowed water to seep in. In the 1950s-1960s a portion of the basement's wood floor was replaced with a hand-mixed concrete foundation. Thereafter, square vinyl tiles were placed on the new floor. *Iglesia La Luz Del Mundo* replaced the entire floor with concrete by 2022 shortly after it purchased the building.

When the early building was raised, a furnace that used a boiler system was probably installed in the basement to replace all the original iron stoves that were used to heat the rooms in the building. These were manually fueled with wood, coal, or coke as was common. If they used a boiler, it was probably covered with asbestos to keep the boiling water percolating hot throughout the system's iron pipes and radiators when these were installed.

I do not recall anyone ever being concerned about contracting the deadly asbestosis illness in the years I worshipped in the building. It was considered the best material in managing heating issues. I do not believe it was the original furnace I saw during the 1950s.

During the winter months, men from the Spanish-speaking Baptist congregation were assigned a weekly task to fire-up the boiler before people arrived on the premises; sometimes the assigned person forgot or could not attend service that morning and a substitute was called to rush to the campus to carry out this critical task.

Without heat in winter, the interior temperature of the building was cold as it was void of insulation throughout. This amenity was rare in building and homes throughout South Chicago during the 19th-20th centuries. Commemorative fresh flowers and potted plants brought into the sanctuary by families to display would freeze overnight during the winter months as thermostats were not used until later years.

In time, the Mexican Baptist congregation replaced the previous furnace. The new one with an automatic ignition system used oil as fuel. In later years, this system was replaced with an automatic system to burn natural gas. A new boiler was installed that did not require asbestos. This system continued to use heated boiling water and iron radiators that had been installed in earlier years.

The accordion-looking iron radiators were of various sizes and ubiquitous throughout the building. They could have been installed when it was raised. Some eight of them were mounted on the basement's east and west walls. Each was a three-tiered radiator unit mounted some ten feet above the floor.

To enhance the heating or cooling of the basement, a medium-sized electric fan in a metal encasement was mounted high over the south end of the room. It was fueled by natural gas and operated by an electric fan which could be manually turned on and off to affect the temperature. A whole-building air conditioning system never existed on the premises between 1885-2021.

During the 1960s and 1970s while people worshiped in the near century-old building, a limited modern forced-air heating system was installed in the basement to mollify the temperature in this room during winter months. It used aluminum ducting that was installed on a section of the east wall. This system was replaced in 2021-2022 by the new owners as said above.

To cool the sanctuary upstairs during hot summer months, two large oscillating electric floor fans were used. Each was mounted to a stainless-steel column attached to a weighted metal base. These were placed throughout the sanctuary. However, a steady humming noise from the motors and whirling fan blades was a challenge to the speakers. Small hand-held fans were often distributed during the summers to anyone who needed one.

The above entire system was replaced by the *Iglesia La Luz Del Mundo* in 2020-2021 when they installed a large new all-building heating, ventilating and air conditioning system which was installed on the exterior east side of their empty lot.

During the years when the Mexican Baptist occupied the building, a small kitchen with a large commercial grade gas stove with multiple burners was located in the southeast area of the basement. In it, the congregation women prepared exciting ethnic and American meals for wedding receptions, birthdays, Easter, Thanksgiving, New Year and other events. The latest congregation has modernized the kitchen and slightly expanded it since they became the new owners.

The building had two inadequate restrooms during the years when *Iglesia Bautista Del Salvador* occupied it. Yet, these were surely an upgraded system to the original 1885 facilities. They were located in the basement near the stairway leading to the building's north entrance. They were probably installed when the building was raised to its current height before the 20th century.

The men's facility was a small room with a step-up floor that had a frosted glass window high on the north and east walls. The women used another adjacent restroom which was slightly larger than the men's and also had a frosted glass window high over the north wall. Both rooms were dimly lit. The only heat in each room came from the heat of the hot water pipes, not radiators, as these passed overhead in the room. In 2021-2022, *Iglesia La Luz Del Mundo* sealed the restroom windows, modernized and relocated these facilities for both genders in the north area of the basement.

On an early Sunday morning in June 2022, I was able to enter the building of *Iglesia La Luz Del Mundo*. At the end of their service, I met Pastor Marcelo Araujo, a leader of the congregation Susie Ortiz Urbina, and a few members. I introduced myself and shared the purpose of my visit to the building. They felt honored to know that a former congregant was interested in writing about the history of the building. They invited me to lunch in the remodeled basement where I provided them more information about my research.

I requested and received permission to tour the building after they had ended a service that day and on the following day. I walked throughout the site to observe the changes I discuss in this book. This congregation is a Spanish-speaking Fundamental Christian Church, and not Baptist nor Roman Catholic. Though it is small, it is a member of a larger organization and is prepared to grow their ministry here. Their leaders have dedicated time, effort and funds to make this house of God beautiful, modern, and functional for years to come in this community.

A little over a year later, in September 2023, I learned that Pastor Araujo accepted a new pastorate assignment in Oceanside, California. I believe his leadership ability has been duly recognized and provided him the opportunity to be transferred to his new pastorate as I stated to him in a telephone call. I wished him success in his new ministry.

New Owners, Old Challenges

After the *Iglesia Bautista Del Salvador* vacated the property[43] in 1991, it appears two non-Hispanic, English-speaking congregations occupied the premises. I took a picture of the building in late October 2017 during one of my visits to the area. I saw a medium unpainted rectangular plywood sign with semi-gothic lettering mounted to the front of the building near the main entrance. It provided the name of the congregation: New Holy Trinity Temple Interdenominational. It also had the design of a Coptic cross painted on the right side and indicates that Elder Carl Winfrey is Founder and Pastor. No other information was provided.

In December 2019 I downloaded information about the building. I located a Coldwater Banker Homes advertisement that announced it had sold the property at 9001 S. Houston Avenue in February of this year for "cash, as is, with no warranties and no repairs." It was selling for an "awesome price" of eighty-thousand dollars. The owner is listed as Restoration Primitive Christian Church. It is unclear whether New Holy Trinity Temple International sold it to this last owner.

I have not researched who either of these English-speaking congregations were. It is difficult to ascertain whether they were the same entity with different names, independent or part of a larger association, their mission, ministry, and any activities they may have had. I am sure both of them did what they could to maintain the building. They had a low profile in the community when compared to the two previous Baptist congregations. The building's exterior reveal serious deterioration was occurring a few years after *Iglesia Bautista Del Salvador* vacated the building. Similar conditions may have been occurring in the interior of the building as well.

In February 2019, the Spanish-speaking congregation, *Iglesia La Luz Del Mundo* bought and assumed possession of the building for less than the ninety-three thousand dollars asking price. Since then, the new owner has invested thousands of dollars beyond the purchase price, to improve this site internally and externally such as I saw in 2022-2023.

Maintaining the exterior of the building was a perennial line-item budget expense for *Iglesia Bautista Del Salvador*. The original wooden north wall was extended some ten to fifteen feet with gray concrete blocks. This extension has never been retouched in any fashion until 2022 when the new owners painted it. The south wall of the church building and a private residence at 9009 S. Houston Avenue, were constructed only inches apart. This house was built in 1894, nine years after the Baptist building was constructed and appears to be in very good condition in 2023.

As a result of the deterioration of the side area where this building almost touches the south wall of the Baptist building, I was able to see the original thin, unpainted wood slats of the Baptist building and how these were later overlain with manufactured rectangular white slate material. This portion of the building has received the least amount of any reconstruction updates, probably because of the closeness of both buildings. In early August 2021, I saw renovation work was being done on this wall which revealed the above condition. It was obvious that this wall would need to and could be improved now that the entire brick chimney was removed when a large heating and air-conditioning unit was installed on the east side of the building sometime in 2021-2022.

Earlier building changes occurred during 1950s-1970s when long aluminum siding looking like wood shiplap was placed over the previous exterior man-made siding. This material covered the south wall, and the upper portions of the east and west exterior walls down to where the foundation touches the base of the wall. The concrete block foundation had remained uncovered for years but was painted in 2019-2021 by the current owners with a gray color to complement the remodeling of the exterior of the building.

By 2017 some aluminum panels had lost their adherence to their two previous covers of the exterior walls, especially on the west or S. Houston Avenue. In late 2018, I saw exterior wall coverings on the south and north entrances were also missing or detached from the structure. Orange-colored warning signs were posted to the two entrances to warn the owner that building repairs needed to be resolved. The exterior appearance gave the building a neglected view to the public.

During a 2019 internet view of the building, I observed that the entire exterior of the building was quite improved since *Iglesia La Luz Del Mundo* acquired it. Some friends who lived in the area and attended the Spanish-speaking services here years ago also informed me that they had seen some exterior work was being done to the exterior of the building. My on-line review confirmed that scaffolds were being used to reach the high walls to work on them. During 2020-2021, the three exterior foundation walls of the basement were smartly painted in a grey-white color as was the block-brick wall on the north side of the building. By 2023 some of the windows on this side of the wall were sealed and painted.

Starting approximately in 2019, the above congregation began making initial improvements to the heating and air conditioning of the building. Initially, small air conditioning units were mounted to one or two sanctuary windows on the S. Houston Avenue side (west side of the building) and the balcony. In August 2021, I noticed the placement of a huge heating and air-conditioning unit that was mounted on a steel structure awaiting installation on the east side of the building and was on its way toward completion. The unit was designed and passes through a part of this wall to service the entire building. I viewed it through the wire fence that surrounds the east parcels. In addition, I saw several square yards of thick, new concrete had been poured over a section of the ground where grass and weeds grew perennially, and the area on which a wooden two-story building once existed on the corner of 90th Street and S. Houston Avenue.

Also, I noticed a newly poured sloping concrete walkway at the northeast corner of the building. It leads to the concrete slab on the east parcels part of the property. The two projects are laudable and will enhance the congregation's ministry by providing adequate heating and cooling as needed, and accessibility to the lot for campus out-of-door events. In addition, the original small, old basement entrance located at southeast ground level had been sealed and replaced by a new double door in the center of the east wall. It will provide easy egress and exit to the basement and the newly paved outside area.

The 1885 Baptist building was originally constructed of wood throughout. Cement block extensions to the north wall, the two building entrances and basement area were added in later years. The building's framework has supported the thirty-foot and perhaps higher walls of the building for one-hundred-and-thirty-eight-years. Its condition has been vastly improved by *Iglesia La Luz Del Mundo* since it purchased the structure.

Though old, the building has always manifested a structural level of integrity. Yet, in order to strengthen it further, sometime in 2019-2021, *Iglesia La Luz Del Mundo* brought a transformation to the building. The basement looks entirely new. A new concrete floor has been poured, and the old knotty, amber-colored pine wall panels were replaced with drywall and painted white. The old support beams appear to have been placed with steel I-beams. New rest rooms for men and women were installed and the kitchen was remodeled as stated above. In addition, the steep north and south stairways to this room have been beautifully improved and partially modified.

As said earlier, the steel radiators throughout the building were removed as a new heating, ventilating and air conditioning unit was recently installed. The congregation has introduced numerous other esthetic, symbolic and functional changes to the sanctuary. This is seen in the image of a river of water seeming to flow in center of the ceiling of the sanctuary. Perhaps it is alluding to the clear river of life referenced in the Book of Revelation, Chapter 22. Other portions in the sanctuary have also been improved since 2019 that complement their worship services.

Membership Directories

In 1926, the congregation of *Iglesia Bautista Del Salvador*[44] was composed of Mexican men, women, and children of all ages. They represented a single immigrant group, first-generation offspring, and emigrants as we have stated before. During the 1950s, other Spanish-speaking ethnic groups became members. Some came and remained, others left. As it grew in membership in the 1950s, I remember discussions about producing a membership directory which could improve communication with the parishioners and other potential uses.

In late May 1965, Pastor Pilar Muñoz produced a mimeographed directory of several pages. It listed the names of forty-four households and other information pertinent to each, i.e., names, addresses, phone number, and birth dates for each household member. I do not think anyone envisioned it would become a valuable document to discuss and support the history of this congregation.

The seventeen-page, 8.5x12 inch document was titled, *Directorio De La Iglesia Bautista El Salvador* (Directory of the El Salvador Baptist Church). It listed the names of seven group leaders or deacons who were assigned a cohort of seven to eight families. Some parishioners remembered that the fortieth anniversary of the congregation was approaching. To celebrate this milestone, I was encouraged by Pastor Salinas to produce an updated membership directory which would be presented in the 1966 celebration.

In order to complete this assignment, I sought assistance from congregants and a faithful former pastor of this congregation, Rev. Balderas who was still active nearby in Christ's work. He was a man of God who loved to preach, teach, write, sing, play the piano, and print documents and reports for the various Baptist organizations in which he was a member and officer. He allowed me the use of his home printing equipment in East Chicago, Indiana.

I produced a new 8.5x9.5 inch 16-page, beige-colored directory in booklet form. It contained a light blue colored silk ribbon with the words, "*40 Aniversario, Iglesia Bautista 'El Salvador' Chicago, Illinois*, with October 13, 1966." As I used Spanish, I should have written, '*Quadragésimo*' and not used the Arabic numbering. I was not corrected by anyone. The inside first page stated, "To the King of ages, immortal, invisible, the only God, be honor and glory for ever and ever. Amen," from I Timothy 1:17.

I referred to it as the Second Edition directory respectful of the earlier work by Pastor Muñoz. It contained the names of sixty families including individual names and other information. I looked forward to the day when it was to be presented to the congregation.

During the Sunday morning service of October 10, 1966, while I was seated at the organ, Pastor Salinas asked me to come to the pulpit and lectern to present the new directory. He made a few remarks about the church's milestone and the effort it must have taken to produce the directory for this anniversary as he held it up. People applauded and I was humbled by this recognition. It was distributed in the morning and evening services that day.

In addition to names, it also contained a brief history about the purchase of the building from First Baptist Church of South Chicago on October 30, 1951, for a sum of $10,000, which I had previously read in other sources. This directory was used until a new one was published some eight years later.

I could not confirm exact tenure dates and names for each of the pastors who served in this congregation. Therefore, I could not determine who was the pastor when the building was purchased. He could have been Godínez, Oliveres, Muñoz, Balderas, or Montemayor.

As stated earlier, the Spanish-speaking congregation was in its heydays of growth during the 1950s-1960s. There was excitement to move forward to either build a new building or expand the existing one. The congregation and leaders envisioned plans to meet its future numerical and evangelistic growth from this location. I remember being asked to draw sketches of what a new or expanded building might look like on our property. Everyone was excited to see what we might be able to do if we had the human and financial resources in addition to our aspirations.

The history of the congregation in the 1966 directory included the purchase price of the property, but no information about three other vacant parcels of land on the east side adjacent to the congregation's two parcels it already owned. Each parcel has the dimensions as what the *Iglesia Bautista Del Salvador* bought in 1951: seventy-five feet wide by one-hundred-and-twenty-five feet long, with elevation of each one below street and sidewalk level. The names of the family members in the three directories may be found in the back of this book.

Three Additional Land Parcels Bought (1965)

In March-April 1965, a research committee was approved by the board of directors of the congregation, thirty-seven-year-old Pastor Salinas and congregation members. They were to investigate the vacant parcels of land[45] for potential purchase. They scheduled a meeting with the Chicago Baptist Association regarding this topic. My personal schedule did not allow me time to participate in this event.

In time, the committee brought their report and findings to a congregation business meeting. I remember attending this evening. After a lengthy discussion, a decision was made on May 8, 1965, to pay $6,340 for the above three parcels including some the delinquent property taxes. Now, the congregation could earnestly proceed to further discuss how to expand or build on the entire five parcels.

Shortly thereafter, in addition to our faith and trust in God, Pastor Salinas and the directors of the congregation wished to meet with the leaders of two large Baptist organizations in Chicago to seek their support. These were the American Baptist Association, with which this congregation was a member for years, and the Southern Baptist Association, a potential alternative supporter. After various meetings with the particular leaders of these organizations, they recommended there was need for congregational growth and organizational areas before they could firmly assist us. Moving forward was going to be a slow process but hope was not lost.

In 1970-1971, a transfer of membership from the American Baptist Association to the Southern Baptist Association was made. This action brought financial support for some of the congregation's budget line items. However, support for a new structure or expansion of the existing building was not realized. This organization offered suggestions to *Iglesia Bautista Del Salvador* similar to what the other Baptist group had made.

The experience was a challenge and a learning opportunity. The congregation proceeded with other achievable building plans which could be easily reached and managed without incurring a huge financial building debt. We knew membership growth was necessary but in the meantime, other action plans could to be taken.

A major benefit to *Iglesia Bautista Del Salvador* was when it purchased the new three adjacent parcels. Now it had the title of ownership of valuable property. Now, *Iglesia Bautista Del Salvador* or any future owner would have access to the entire location without any land constraints to expand or build a new structure.

Around this time, Pastor Salinas resigned after having served here for some five years. Thereafter, Pastor Muñoz was appointed as an interim pastor with other ministers who assisted and diligently served in this capacity for some four years until a permanent pastor was chosen.

In 1974, a six-page 5.5"x8.5" membership directory was published on pink colored paper. Though incomplete, it served its purpose as did previous editions. Pastor Domingo Ozuna was appointed the new leader of the congregation. He was accompanied by his wife, Dolores. Membership had diminished to less than fifty families, with a list for potential growth by families who were considering new members or renewing their membership. Member's names and our men who were serving in the U.S. Military Service during the above years are listed the back of this book.

Sometime in 1974 I received a letter that said I was eligible for a full-time post-graduate fellowship at Southern Illinois University, in Carbondale, Illinois. I had previously applied for this program and now I had to decide. After discussions with my wife, family and friends, and Pastor Ozuna, I accepted this opportunity and moved. Upon arriving I enrolled in the Graduate School of Education. Shortly thereafter, I learned that Pastor Ozuna had resigned his position with plans to return to work in a ministerial position in Texas.

I received my Ph.D. on a spring morning of May 14, 1976. My wife, three daughters and family members witnessed this event. A few days later I returned to Chicago upon being appointed as an administrator and faculty member at Chicago State University.

Building Signage

Throughout the history of this building, signage has always been seen in pictures taken of the façade of the building. We first see one in a photograph taken circa 1885 shortly after it was built. We see a small, almost unnoticeable sign attached to the left corner of the building near the original north entrance. Though illegible, it may have displayed the name of the congregation. It appears unilluminated, probably painted black and may have used gold-colored letters which was traditionally seen in church building signage[46] of that time.

The sign was enlarged as seen in later photos. The wooden frame was made in an ecclesiastical design and provided limited information about the congregation and related announcements.

Up until 1951 when the Mexican congregation bought the building the previous sign was flush with the exterior on the west wall near the north entrance. It was modified to announce service times, dates, and sermon title, which was commonly posted information. It did not provide the church's telephone number nor the name of the pastor.

After the Spanish-speaking Baptist congregation purchased the building the sign was slightly changed. It was mounted in the same location as the previous one. It was a medium size rectangular wood box, painted black, with a small glass covered door. To update information, a person had to place a ladder on sidewalk on the west side of the building to reach the box, unlatch its door, and manually insert moveable white plastic letters and numerals into the grooves with the current information.

Sometime during 1963-1964, the signage was totally replaced and simplified by a new larger and modern one. It projected away from the northwest corner of the building on S. Houston Avenue. It was made of white translucent plastic and lit from within with fluorescent light tubes. It displayed, *"IGLESIA BAUTISTA Bienvenidos"* (Baptist

Church Welcome) in black and white lettering. This sign was later removed and replaced with another one constructed of metal and plastic material with exterior electric spotlight lamps attached to both sides for nighttime illumination. It hung in place for several years.

When *Iglesia Bautista Del Salvador* vacated the building in 1991, the sign was replaced by the Primitive Christian Church or whomever was the successor congregation. I did not find any signs on the building with this name. Another congregation, as discussed above, New Holy Trinity Temple leaders installed a sign with their name on it. It was a simple one about four feet long by two feet wide on inch thick wood. The sign was attached flat to the wall on the S. Houston Avenue side to the right of the north entrance of the building. It remained here throughout the duration of their occupancy and then removed sometime after they vacated it.

In 2019-2020, *Iglesia La Luz Del Mundo* replaced this sign with a simple new rectangular wooden one about the same size as the one discussed above. It is painted in large letters on a black background. It can be seen today on the remodeled exterior west wall where the signs have always been mounted.

Interior Beautification

In 1976, the men of the Spanish-speaking Baptist congregation executed a new project[47] to paint the interior walls of the sanctuary and lobby and refurbish the oak floor. I had recently completed my doctoral studies and returned to South Chicago after a two-year absence. I was chosen to collaborate with the other men to move this project forward. This activity is referenced in the program notes of the fifty-first anniversary in 1977.

To complete the above project, all morning, evening, and Wednesday night services in the sanctuary were cancelled for a month. In the interim, these were celebrated in the basement. The project seemed to take longer than this for some congregants. To facilitate our project, we rented metal tubed scaffolds and assembled them along the interior walls. All the furniture and accessories were moved within the room: pews, chairs, and hymnals. The soft pink carpet in the three aisles was removed. The ebony colored Chickering grand piano and Hammond organ were covered with drop cloths and minimally moved.

We completed painting the walls and proceeded to dismantle the scaffolds and began to paint the imbedded metal wall radiators with a silver color. Once this was completed, we proceeded to sand and refurbish the entire sanctuary's scuffed oak wood floor.

To accomplish this, we rented a round industrial size electric floor sander and began this task. We soon learned that the electrical system in the building was inadequate to provide sufficient amperage to continuously operate the sander. After many starts and stops, the floor sanding was finished and we proceeded to minimally sand the pews.

The next step was to return these and the other furniture we had moved to their proper location. Placing the pews to their correct place was like working a giant jigsaw floor puzzle which we had not considered beforehand. They were of different lengths and needed to be perfectly aligned and centered on the floor, while leaving an aisle on the east and west sides, and a wider one in the center of the room. We also had to place the pulpit furniture to their proper location. The carpet was replaced sometime after all the other work was finished. We thanked God that we had no accidents while we worked on this major project.

No outside contractor was hired on the aforesaid project. The men who volunteered were proud that our work had saved the congregation thousands of dollars to make beautiful the sanctuary of this House of God. The building was not as beautiful as King Solomon's temple in Jerusalem which was filled with gold, silver, and precious stones and did not contain a Holy of Holies inner room, but it was beautiful in its own right when finished. Once this project was complete, it was several years later that other project such as this one was scheduled. Some of these are discussed elsewhere in this history.

One of our congregants observed what we were doing and wished to thank us. Brother Pedro A. Ruíz, one of our in-house wordsmith poets and husband of Belén Ruíz, wrote a nine-verse quatrain poem, "*Nuestra Iglesia* (Our Church)," to commemorate this project. Though this beautiful couple have left this earth, Pedro's words compared our building to a beautiful site built in an oasis. He said this building was where a tired sojourner would come to rest and drink of its fresh water, enjoy the hospitality, and find God. The words captured brother ' gift in expressing his thoughts in Spanish. He wrote other beautiful pieces like this in other historic events throughout his lifetime.

Maintaining the overall integrity of the building was always a challenge due its age and wear over the years. An important safety structural improvement had to be added sometime during the 1960s when two or three round, two-inch, steel rods were professionally installed in the sanctuary and were readily observable by all. These were needed to strengthen and keep the building's east and west walls from imploding. These were ultimately obscured when a false ceiling was installed in this room in the late 1960s when the lancet windows were also removed. The rods were subsequently removed in 2020-2021 by *Iglesia La Luz Del Mundo* during the reconstruction of the entire building.

Sometime during 1970-1980, a section of the sanctuary's original plaster ceiling collapsed into the room just before a major event was scheduled to take place. The room was unavailable for services until the ceiling was repaired. This damage is noted in the fifty-third anniversary Program in 1979, along with other historic church milestones reached.

Interior Description

During the decades when *Iglesia Bautista Del Salvador* owned the building, the sanctuary was divided into two main sections[48]. Each had nine rows of pine hewn pews, which comfortably accommodated at least ten adults each. In the mid-1950s, some discarded old pew cushions were found in various parts of the building which had been used by the previous congregation. These were never replaced though some people thought they should have to soften the stress of sitting on the hard pews. An estimate of the width of each of the aisles on the east and west side of the room was some twenty inches. The center aisle was some thirty-six-inches wide and abutted with the pulpit. The east aisle ran the length of the room and abutted with the pulpit to the left of the baptistry. The west aisle ran the length of the room and ended at the upper beginning of the stairwell leading to the basement.

The interior height of the room from the wooden floor to the apex of the unobstructed slanted ceiling was some twenty-five to thirty feet. The twelve historic lancet stained-glass windows lined the east and west walls of the sanctuary. A stairway ran along the east wall and could be accessed from the south entrance. The other was located in the center and back area (north) of the room and was accessed from S. Houston Avenue at the north corner. Both entrances and stairways allowed easy access and egress to the sanctuary. The stairs were hewn of oak wood and uncarpeted and creaked when people walked on them. The bannisters in these had to be firmly grasped for one's personal safety due to the steep angle of the stairways.

In addition to the sanctuary, there were two small rooms behind the pulpit area wall. The east was generally used as a classroom. The west room was often used as pastor's office and had a quaint fireplace in one of the corners. A small open cloak area in the back of the sanctuary was where people could leave their hats, coats, umbrellas, and snow boots during the winter months while in the building. None of these rooms nor the baptistry exist today as described above. The walls on the north and south ends of the room have changed the configuration of this wide floor.

In 1885, when the building was constructed, under the north part of the roof, a medium-sized balcony was included. When the building was reconstructed in the 19th century, it was redesigned with a room having three regular sized rectangular windows inserted into the roof facing east. The English-speaking congregation used this room for many purposes. Its entrance door on the first floor had a phrase painted on it with the words, "Born Again," indicating it was where believers came to learn about their faith, Bible studies, or praying in a small group setting.

Sometime after *Iglesia Bautista Del Salvador* assumed ownership of the building, this phrase was replaced with "*El Aposento Alto* (the Upper Room)." The room served for various purposes throughout the week similar to the ones stated above. To mollify the sound in the room while in use, during the 1970s, it was sealed off with a transparent plastic shield that ran from the east to the west wall. It continued from a short wall in the room up to the ceiling. The room seemed to float over the interior of the sanctuary where the people sitting below in the pews could be seen and minimally heard depending on the activity being held in either room.

During the 1960s-1970s, a portion of this medium-sized balcony was divided into a small chapel which had two plastic stained-glass windows mounted onto two of its temporary short walls. it was designed to enhance the use of the *Aposento Alto*. However, due to inadequate heating and cooling, and accessibility to the balcony via two steep stairways, it was minimally used. The greater part of this room continued to be used by the youth Bible study group discussed later in this document.

In 2022, I saw the balcony was partially sealed with drywall in the north hallway. A door with windows revealed that part of this space was now being used for an office and other purposes. A stairway on the west side and outside of this room is where four beautiful small arched stained-glass windows are seen. These were installed when the original building was extended northward.

For over a hundred years, the balcony which faced east revealed rows of chimneys which were part of the U.S. Steel industry. Viewers could see the atmosphere being filled with long toxic rainbow-colored plumes of residual smoke as thousands of tons of steel were being produced on the mill's lakeshore premises. This industrial scene began to fade in the 1970s when steelmaking corporate leaders announced the beginning of the end of this industry where thousands of men and women worked, with some being from both Baptist congregations, including some relatives. The actual end came in the early 1980s.

Entrance View

The building we see today has two double-door wooden entrances[49] on S. Houston Avenue. One is on the north corner and another on the south of the building.

When the structure was extended on the north end, gray colored concrete stonework surrounded the doorway. It was enclosed by fluted columns on either side in Doric architectural style. A long rectangular lintel is found over it which enhances the façade. This beautiful design remains in 2023 with little modification.

For decades, the north doors were imbedded with small-lancet-shaped windows. Old photographs of the doors show their design was introduced when the building was raised and extended. Over the decades, the doors were replaced with new ones with different designs. In 2020-2021, *Iglesias La Luz Del Mundo* replaced the ones that had beautiful semi-circular glass windows in them with new wood double doors and small rectangular windows.

In a photo dated 1945, sent to me in 2021 by Theresa Martínez, I was able to see part of the beautiful horizontal half-circle window over the north entryway. Standing to the right side, we see a young Adela Pérez Gonsález, wife of Jesús Gonsález, posing for the picture. The entire window above Adela is not shown, but I was able to see a partial name, First Baptist Church of South Chicago, embedded into the lower part of the leaded stained glass.

The rest of the window had an image of a dove emerging from the white rays and clouds, surrounded by a globe and other rays bursting within the window, including an image of a cross. These are historic Christian symbols of the dove representing Christ; the Holy Spirit; the globe, the World, and the empty cross, Christ's crucifixion and resurrection.

Sometime in the mid-1950s, I recall the leaders of *Iglesia Bautista Del Salvador* modified the stained glass design. It was replaced with gold-colored stained-glass with a cross made of darker colored panes embedded in the center, sans the name of the Spanish-speaking congregation. It was illuminated by an incandescent light bulb hanging within the small interior space over the door. I remember the bulb had to be replaced occasionally. I volunteered to do this several times and found it a dusty but needed chore.

Also, immediately above this window, are four small unopenable arched stained-glass windows which face west. Each is configured in yellow, with a diamond shaped center surrounded by strips of pink, and tan glass along the frame of each window. In June 2022, though extant, I only took a picture of three of these located in the stairway leading to the balcony and is shown in this book.

In 2020-2021, I saw the half-circle window above the door had been entirely sealed by *Iglesia La Luz Del Mun*do with plywood and painted over with a color that matches the exterior of the building. This action supports this denomination's religious beliefs regarding the use of some symbols. It reminds me of the small stained-glass windows in the Agudath Achim Bikur Cholim Synagogue which had Jewish symbols and words embedded in them. These were also covered over by one of the succeeding congregations.

Three other unopenable smaller arched stained glass windows are extant. They are found high above the north wall around the corner of the main entrance. They were part of the extension of the building probably introduced sometime in the 20th century.

Facilitator in Establishing the First Mexican Baptist Church in South Chicago

L-R, Frank and Elisa Pérez, friend, and Amelia Balderas at the 100th birthday for Mary Martínez, in Hammond, Indiana, circa July 2013. Faithful Christians for decades. (Source, Theresa Martínez, 2014.)

(L to R) Deacons Cruz Quiñones and Ramón Martínez prepare to collect tithes and offerings. Note an arched window, pulpit, piano cover and its side, large sculptured lectern, and the top of a electronic cross in the baptistry. (Béloz. Circa, 1967.)

The First Baptist Church of South Chicago

Above, an early image of the immigrant-built shiplap siding structure of First Baptist Church of South Chicago circa 1885, at the corner of S. 90th and Houston Avenue. A man is standing on the wooden sidewalk (right) could be the first pastor of the congregation and the other thirteen people could be parishioners. This section will be extended northward, the entrance will be changed, the tower will be removed and the building raised. (Southeast Chicago Historical Society, 2022).

Facilitator in Establishing the First Mexican Baptist Church in South Chicago

The north side of building (left) was extended by adding the half-moon window and four smaller ones, and the bell tower was removed. The original 13 arched stained-glass windows on the first floor were removed circa 1968-70 while the Mexican congregation occupied it. After they closed, one or two non-Spanish speaking congregations occupied it. When the last one left, it was vacant for a while and the owners used plywood to protect the windows. In 2019, a realtor listed the building for sale, "as is" and waited for a buyer. *Iglesia La Luz Del Mundo* bought it as shown and later reduced the number of windows and covered the half-moon window in 2021-2022. (Béloz.)

The building was purchased in 2019-2020 by *Iglesia La Luz Del Mundo*. They have made major improvements to the premises: fewer and smaller windows, installed a complete HVAC system, rain gutters, and other interior improvements. While it is no longer a Baptist Church it is committed to His work in South Chicago for years to come. (Béloz, 2022.)

The First Baptist Church of South Chicago

The simple interior of *Iglesia Bautista Del Salvador* sanctuary sans the stained-glass windows. They were located on the left and right side walls. This basic scene lasted for almost sixty-six years after it was purchased in 1953. Note the pulpit and chairs, lectern, organ sound unit, baptistry with a lighted cross, and a door leading to a Sunday School room. A picture below shows some datails.
(Béloz, 1966.)

Sanctuary of *Iglesia Bautista Del Salvador* circa mid-1960s, before all the stained glass windows and imbeded memorials at the bottom of each were removed. The Hammon Organ console, radiators and pews are seen in this northwest view. The back and top of the lecturn are seen on the right. (Beloz, 1966.)

Facilitator in Establishing the First Mexican Baptist Church in South Chicago

The same room as above. All lancet stained-glass windows on the east and west walls were removed. The high ceiling was lowered with a faux one, with imbedded fluorescent lights. Anita Fierro is seated at the Chickering piano (left), and Élida Aceves is seated in a pew on the right side. (Béloz, 1971.)

Current design of the sanctuary by the new owners *Iglesia La Luz Del Mundo*. (2022). Note the height of the ceiling and submerged lights, pulpit and simple window design. (Béloz, 2023.)

One of the earliest photos of the *Convención Bautista Hispano-Americana*, taken in 1928, two years after it was founded in South Chicago. The site is unknown. Mrs. Mary Martinez is the woman seated in the left side of the photo, third row. Some information is taken from notes on the back of the photo I received in August 2020 from Martínez family.

The First Baptist Church of South Chicago

11th *Convención Bautista Hispano Americana*, held in South Chicago, 1937. Mary Martínez, Rev. Pilar Muñoz, and other conventioneers are seen. (Mary Martínez.)	10th *Convención, Bautista Hispana Americana*, in Kansas City, Missouri, 1936 This was Mary Martínez' tenth annual meeting (left edge, fourth row). (Mary Martínez.)

Rev. Pilar and Elizabeth Muñoz (left), Rev. M. Castillo, Rev. J. Thome (left, front), Rev. J. Macías and other pastors and conventioneers attend the 50th annual *Convención Bauista Hispano Americana* in Indiana, 1978. Known family surnames include Béloz, López, Manzo, Martínez, Vásquez and others. (Roby Muñoz, 1978.)

Facilitator in Establishing the First Mexican Baptist Church in South Chicago

The 25th *Convención Bautista Hispano Americana* in front of our church building, June 23-28, 1951. Rev. Basil, Williams and several other pastors who served in this church and in the Convención leadership are seen. Recognizable families include Armas, Fierro, Gonsález, López, Manzo, Marcano, Meadows, Mendoza, Pérez and others. Note the two church signs. The window over the entrance to building was sealed in 2022. (Mary Martínez.)

The First Baptist of South Chicago moved to this new building in 1952-1953 after *Iglesia Bautista Mexicana* purchased it. After fifty-eight years here, they moved to a larger building and later became Compassion Baptist Church of Chicago. (Béloz, 2023.)

Iglesia Bautista Del Salvador parishioners with Pastor Rev. Humberto Salinas, his wife, Socorro, and sons Benjamín and Nehemías recall the 40th decade anniversary (1970s). Families present include Aceves, Armas, Bautista, Béloz, Briones, Cendejas, Evans, Fierro, López, Pérez, and Vásquez. The half-moon and four small windows above were additions to the 1885 building. The larger one was sealed in 2022 by the current owners of the building. (Béloz)

The First Baptist Church of South Chicago

Rev. Carlos M. Gurrola. Our second pastor during the early 1920s. (*Convención Bautista.com.*)

Rev. Moisés López, pastor during the late 1960s-70s. Ordained here after years of service. Note cedar panel walls in our church's basement. (Béloz.)

Rev. Domingo Ozuna and wife, Dolores. Probably our only living pastor from 1974. (Ozuna, 2022.)

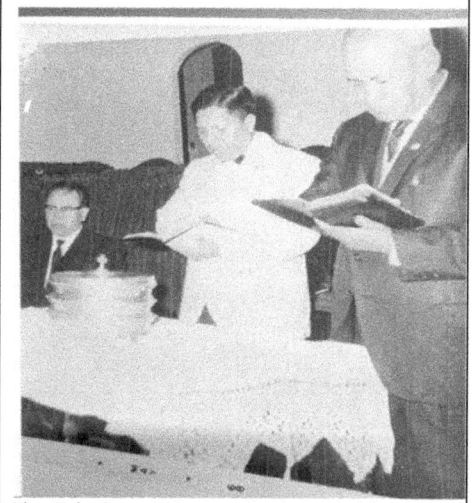

The Holy Communion service being led by Pastor Rev. Humberto Salinas (center), Deacon Jesús Gonsález (left) and former pastor Rev. Pilar Muñoz, May, 1968. Note the silver service tray which contain the communion elements and the table covering. (Béloz, 1968.)

Left photo below: Ladies group, Mary Martínez (back, right corner), Lupe López, Ángela Mendoza, Ignacia Rivera, Dolores Manzo, Esther Montemayor, Eunice Fierro, Ángelina Pérez, Ángela Mendoza, Adela Gonsález and son, Paul, Dolores Fierro, and other women from this church. (Mary Martnez)

Right photo: Mary Martínez on her 100th birthday party with family members, Hammond, Indiana, July, 2014. Mary's Christian service in this Baptist church began in the 1920s until her passing shortly after this photo was taken. (Theresa Martínez, 2014.)

The Sanctuary Pulpit

The Baptist Church's sanctuary pulpit[50] we saw for many years was modified over the decades. Original architectural plans or photos of this room might clarify changes that may have been made to it. I believe it was not part of the original design in 1885. It may have been slightly above the floor. An anomaly was created when a larger and higher pulpit was installed. As a result, the bottom of the windowsills on the pulpit and the bottom of the southwest classroom floor abut without any space between them. I noticed this anomaly as I would walk up the stairs to the pulpit using the east stairway.

During the years when I worshipped here, the pulpit was made of wood, three feet high and almost the width of the room but shorter on stage left (west). Access to it was by walking up carpet-covered low stairways located on both sides of the pulpit. Short dark pink velvet curtains supported by brass rings and tubing were mounted on the front of the pulpit floor. These were movable items.

A large, beautiful sculptured, wood lectern was always placed in the center of the pulpit as were all previous ones. I recall that someone painted a grey colored cross in its center which could readily be seen by the audience. On one occasion, the lectern was placed on stage left and there was unfavorable murmuring until it was replaced to its "proper place" per Baptist tradition. Pastors delivered sermons from here, sometimes wearing an ecclesiastical black robe or business attire. Speakers also used the lectern when the pulpit was being used for other programs. The American flag was always placed stage right. The tri-colored Christian flag with its small red cross within the blue canton was placed stage left, near the Hammond organ.

Today, *Iglesia La Luz Del Mundo* has built a larger and higher pulpit. It is very attractive and meets the congregation's tradition in its religious services and other programs.

Holy Communion Sacrament (*la Santa Cena*)

When I began attending *Iglesia Bautista Del Salvador*, a small communion table was being used[51]. Years later, it was replaced by a newer one. It was about three feet high, made of mahogany with four carved legs with a drawer in the back. The Frank Pérez family claimed it and "el mantel" (white communion tablecloth cover) in 1991 when the Spanish-speaking Baptist congregation vacated the building. The latter has the words, "*Dios es amor*" knit into it one of the two versions of the mantel. These are the only artifacts of the Holy Communion that were used and are extant. David Pérez retains the table. His sister María Teresa Pérez and Elisa Pérez each possess one of two manteles for safekeeping.

Iglesia Bautista Del Salvador celebrated Holy Communion (la Santa Cena) on the first Sunday of the month during the 7 p.m. service, for years. During the 1960s-1970, after a business meeting vote, it was changed to be celebrated on the first Sunday of the month, during the 11:00 a.m. service, when more parishioners attended. I recall the change was an uncomfortable transition for some but was embraced overall as the months passed.

To participate in this sacrament, the communicant had to have met certain stipulations. These were to have been baptized by full submersion in water in this or any other Baptist congregation or similar faith-believing body, and to conscientiously examine their life and found themselves spiritually prepared to receive this sacrament. Also, with regard to the two Communion elements, the Baptist doctrine does not uphold the belief of transubstantiation of the juice, nor the bread upon being taken in this commemorative service. This belief is held worldwide by most Protestant and Evangelical faiths. The sacrament reminds believers of their faith, obedience, Christ's crucifixion and resurrection and the believer's hope for tomorrow.

Two different plates and memorial elements were used to serve the people seated in the pews during this service. Both were round and made of silver-plated metal or plastic. The first plate had small holes in its interior layer designed to hold small cups filled with grape juice. Wine was never used in this sacrament. It represents the blood of Christ shed for the salvation of humankind. The second contained small wafers or pieces of bread which represent the broken body of Christ.

Both plates were placed on the communion table and covered by *"el mantel"*. The deacons removed it just before the pastor, or a designee raised a dedicatory prayer to God for this Holy service. The elements were served to the communicants seated in the pews.

Upon being served the bread or wafer from the first plate, the element was consumed immediately and the plate passed along to the next communicant. This person then took the second element, the juice, consumed and replaced the cup into the plate, and passed it to the next person. Sometimes, the communicant held the elements briefly to meditate and then consumed it but passed the plate along. Empty cups were placed in small holder in the pew ahead of them. After both elements were distributed, communicants were encouraged to take time to pray and consider the significance of this service.

Occasionally, a variation of the above process was when the pastor invited the communicants to come forward to the communion table to receive the two elements. The pastor or deacon raised a prayer to God and the communicants took the bread and the juice from their respective plates. Thereafter, the communicants would return to their pew to pray and quietly wait until all had participated in this service.

Upon completion of this service, the pastor, deacon or assigned congregant would come to the communion table where the plates for receiving the tithes and offerings were placed. The pastor would raise a prayer of thanksgiving to God and these were distributed to those in the pews who wished to participate could do so. Afterwards, the plates were returned to the communion table and the rest of the service would continue. Upon conclusion of the entire service, the offering plates would be gathered by the deacons assigned to this responsibility for fiscal control and reporting at a later time. Also, the communion plates were covered and removed from the table later by the deacons or deaconesses or designated persons.

Baptism Sacrament

Hundreds of people were baptized in this edifice's baptistry by the pastors of First Baptist Church of South Chicago, and *Iglesia Bautista Del Salvador* for decades. The pastor was the officiant in celebrating this sacrament. I have no information or photographs to confirm where the original location of the baptistry was in the sanctuary in 1885.

When I became a member here in the mid-1950s, the baptistry was located along the south wall of the sanctuary in a small arched alcove. It remained here until 1991 when this congregation closed its doors. It was constructed of a water-tight tin rectangular metal container, about five feet long, three feet wide, and three feet deep.

It was manually filled with tepid water delivered through pipes from the furnace and boiler system located in the basement of the building. It was continuously topped-off with water in anticipation of baptism celebrations.

The front area of the baptistry was surrounded by a clear low glass shield for the parishioners to be able to see the baptismal candidate. Embedded into the wall of the alcove was a small red neon fluorescent glass tube configured in a cross. I have no history as to when this light was installed. It was turned on during all services and baptisms.

Sometime in the 1950s, a young Moisés Briones, nephew of Ángela Briones and Sebastián Pérez, painted a colored oil mural on the back wall of the baptistry alcove. Later on, it had to be replaced and another artist was commissioned to restore it. The result depicted a slight difference between both renditions of a bucolic scene of a river flowing around a cross, through a forest, and seeming to empty into the baptistry. By 2022, the alcove and baptistry were eliminated when the sanctuary was vastly remodeled by *Iglesia La Luz Del Mundo*. In early January 2024, I spoke with the now ninety-seven year old painter and we recalled his artwork he executed decades before.

The sacrament of baptism brings the person into the worldwide family of all other believers in Christ. It was a celebration in which the person of understanding, and after having received counseling and Christian education would be baptized. On a given date the candidate would go to a dressing room where they changed clothes and donned a white robe. Upon being ready, the person walked barefoot into the baptistry filled with water and was met by the pastor who was wearing a white robe over his clothes, and long rubber boots.

Once in the water, the pastor would state the candidate's name and ask if he or she promised to be an example and follower of Jesus Christ for the rest of their life. Upon replying affirmatively, the pastor would say, "I baptize you in the name of the Father, the Son, and the Holy Spirit" and was immediately submerge and quickly raised out of the water. This action symbolized the death of the old person and resurrection and commitment into a new life in Christ and His life-giving spirit.

Christians believe angels in heaven rejoice when a person is baptized[52]. The person would return to the dressing room to dry off and don their clothes. At the end of the service, the person would come forward, receive a certificate of baptism which indicated membership in the congregation and be welcomed into the family of God.

The record of the baptism was entered into the congregation's archives by the church secretary. This action was also reported in the minutes of the next general business meeting. It was also submitted to the Baptist Association offices which recorded and published periodic reports to its member churches.

I doubt printed signs with Bible verses or Christian expressions were seen on the walls of the sanctuary of First Baptist Church of South Chicago before Mexican families began to share the building. However, they were commonly posted on the back wall of the pulpit while *Iglesia Bautista Del Salvador* occupied the building beginning in 1953. I recall one was located above the baptistry's arched lintel in Gothic lettering. It proclaimed, "*Jesús Es El Señor* (Jesus Is Lord)." Other such signs were occasionally posted on the pulpit wall to celebrate special events throughout the years. A small wooden cross was hung on this wall and is seen in the picture of the sanctuary shown here.

I am unaware whether any of the other owners of the Baptist building in South Chicago used the baptistry after 1991 when the Spanish-speaking congregation left. I understand the current owners *Iglesia La Luz Del Mundo* baptizes its members but am not aware of their traditions or other stipulations. While in the building in June 2022, I observed the area where the baptistry alcove used to be located had been sealed, as was the door to the classroom on the right side of the pulpit. Also, the entire sanctuary has been painted in pure white.

I also saw other items in the sanctuary. An image of a wandering stream of blue water runs most of the length of the sanctuary ceiling. Dozens of small lights are imbedded in rows in the ceiling. Each oak pew has a small white figure symbolizing flames attached to its side which must have an important meaning for those who worship here. A white wooden box at the front of the pulpit is probably used for placing one's tithes and offerings at designated times during their services.

Music In the Services

Traditionally, Baptist congregational singing[53] is spirit-filled in their services in which traditional Christian hymns are sung. *Iglesia Bautista Del Salvador* generally sang in Spanish, though English was used in some services in later years. Singing was usually accompanied by the piano, organ, or both.

I firmly believe that our congregants supported the propositions I found in the Foreword of, *The Celebration Hymnal of Songs and Hymns for Worship,* and its definition of singing based on four moving Biblical references as expressed in this text:

"Song is the climate[54] in which God Himself works in His most glorious ways as Creator; Song is the companion means by which we are taught to see the Word of God enriched in its workings within our lives, in practice and purity; Song is the conduit by which the soul's night of darkness is ignited with hope and deliverance; Song is the claim of the barren, by which God says we may entertain and expect fruitfulness, and Song is the conquering instrument available when we are outnumbered by circumstances."

In essence, the songs we sang revealed all of these propositions in our congregational singing, solos or duets. Even today people feel uplifted after praising God through singing a hymn or song which raise one's spirits through the lyrics being expressed within the piece.

When I began attend this church, I remember seeing a piano and a small organ that the English-speaking and Mexican congregation used in their services. I cannot recall when this organ was removed but the piano was retained.

Two instruments were the focal point of the music history of *Iglesia Bautista Del Salvador*. A shiny ebony, nine-foot-long Chickering grand piano was used in nearly all our services and programs. It is very likely this majestic instrument was the one used in the services of First Baptist Church of South Chicago. I once found its serial number which was imprinted on the piano case under its cover. The manufacturer printed it here to document when it was made. I believe this one was made during the 1890s. I saw such a number while it was being fully restrung and restored sometime in the late 1950s. I was responsible to have it tuned at least once biannually. I was always amazed at its clear resonance and its integrity in pitch between and after tunings.

It was accompanied by a dark oak wood adjustable round stool which could be raised to the height needed by the pianist. The beauty of this piece was its design. It had four tapered wooden legs with four metal eagle talon clamps found at the end of each. Each talon grasped a medium sized round clear glass ball. This design was commonly used on various pieces of fine furniture during the Victorian era.

First Baptist Church of South Chicago may have purchased this item new from any of the several music stores in downtown Chicago which sold these instruments and accessories. I believe the piano was the one I first played here in the mid-1950s.

No history of the piano is available, but it was perennially seen and used in the sanctuary for hundreds of services throughout the life of both Baptist congregations. The piano and stool remained in the building when *Iglesia Bautista Del Salvador* vacated the site in 1991. Anecdotes were that the piano and accoutrements were later sold or discarded in the trash. I saw no piano or any musical instruments anywhere in the building when I was in it in June 2022.

The second musical instrument which was considered important to *Iglesia Bautista Del Salvador's* services was having a pipe or electronic organ in the sanctuary. In those decades, this instrument was commonly found in most Baptist churches as were pianos. I recall discussions about purchasing a new one after the previous one was removed. Buying a pipe organ seemed untenable due to the cost and someone available with the ability to play it. After several meetings, a decision was made that an electronic organ would be adequate and a parishioner was available who could play the piano and it.

I have a file which indicates that in July 1954, a mahogany wood spinet electronic dual-manual Hammond organ and standalone speaker unit were purchased for $1,836, payable at $51 in 36 monthly installments. This project launched in faith and wise planning. Our treasurer prepared an all-congregation spread sheet which listed each group that was responsible to make the monthly payment to reduce the debt. Monthly fundraisers were joyously organized by the women to sell *tamales* they prepared in the building's kitchen. These and other projects and personal pledges were also made and the debt was summarily paid in full before the three-year contract was due.

The organ was a beautiful piece of furniture. It had two manuals and was uncomplicated. The unit was an effective instrument in our small sanctuary. It had a host of black and white drawbars placed over the two manuals. An instructions book showed the player how to slide these in or out to produce an expansive range of pipe organ voicings. A group of preset buttons could be used to produce pipe organ or percussion sounds and rhythms. A Leslie unit beautifully enhanced the sound as well.

The organ used vacuum tubes which had to be replaced as needed. The motor had to be oiled once annually. I did this using a special organ lubrication which I purchased in the Lyon & Healy music store in downtown Chicago.

The organ also had buttons to produce various reverberations to accompany soloist or congregational singing. A full scale of foot pedals enriched the organ's bass sound. The volume of the instrument was controlled using a single foot pedal. When the organ and the grand piano were played simultaneously or alone, we heard uplifting sounds in our services, weddings, funerals, memorials, anniversaries or other programs.

The volume of the organ's sound was augmented by a speaker located at the lower back center of the console. A second speaker was bought to increase the volume in the sanctuary. It was placed in the east corner on the pulpit across the room, next to a long, stained-glass lancet-styled window. It was enclosed in a medium size wooden mahogany unit connected to the organ via a long black electric cord. The instrument remained in the building when *Iglesia Batista Del Salvador* vacated the premises and discarded or sold by whomever occupied the building thereafter as stated above.

Several members of this congregation were pianist. During the 1950s-1960s, Larry Autry, a young, tall, African American became a member here. He was an employee in one of the clinics at the University of Chicago, and a very accomplished pianist. He easily adapted to playing the organ and served here for a couple of years. When he moved away, I became the next pianist who transitioned to playing the organ by practicing a few hours on Saturday mornings when the building was vacant. I served as the organist for a total of some six years. A Paul González would accompany me on the piano at times. While I served in the military service (1961-1963), a young member, Ralph Quiñones, served as organist until I returned. He later joined the Air Force.

Dinah Pérez was another young musician. She is the daughter of Antonio and Rhoda Pérez who were leaders in the congregation for many years. Dinah was in her early days of studying to play the piano and often shared her ability as she played solo or accompanied the organ. She played quite competently here for several years. She currently lives and works in California with her husband, Jerry Lockhart.

Christian Education

Sunday was the busiest day of the week during the decades in which *Iglesia Bautista Del Salvador* worshipped God in this building. Its four major activities were: Sunday School (*Escuela Dominical*), a general morning service (*Servicio Matutino*), a youth service (*Los

Jóvenes) which preceded the Sunday evening service (*el culto de noche.*)

Four Christian education[55] classes comprised Sunday School. Each met in the various rooms throughout the building. Three were offered in English and one in Spanish. Sunday School launched the Sunday morning activities.

All the classes operated from 9:00 a.m. to 10:45 a.m. People generally used their personal vehicles to attend. Many walked to the campus if they lived in the local area. In the 1970s, a limited bus ministry was operated. A large yellow bus was used to expand our outreach to the community. It was an exciting ministry for a few years.

Christian education is fundamental to worldwide Evangelical and a Baptist tradition. It is known as Sunday School or Bible School. In *Iglesia Bautista Del Salvador*, this program and its classes were very important in helping the congregants of all ages to understand the teachings and theology found within the Holy Scriptures. In Sunday School we learned that the Bible is composed of sixty-six distinct but related books.

The Old Testament has thirty-nine, and the New Testament has twenty-seven books. Using a broad brush to understand this subject, we learned that the whole Bible has some seven generally accepted major divisions beginning with the first Book of the Bible, Genesis, that God is one entity. The Bible is one book of the continuous story of humanity in relation to God. It provides predictions concerning the future and their fulfillment. Its narrative provides a description of God inspired events or historic stories. It testifies to one redemption for humanity. The entire Bible has one theme in its entire narrative from the first book Genises to the last one, Revelation.

Through the centuries, God inspired many writers to produce a harmonious and unfolding doctrine that has meaning for the believers from thousands of years ago and stands today. We were taught that the Christian believer's understanding and reading of the Bible is to be continuous and not static in order to receive its full meaning and value to one's life. We learned that this belief does not come by osmosis or inherited. Rather, it is to be a personal, daily and active action.

Sunday School classes also taught about Christianity and Baptist tradition. We learned about the significance of one's personal salvation, love for others, the Holy Trinity, the role of the Believers of witnessing and ministering to all about Christ and His love. We also learned about the Ordinance of Baptism by immersion following Christ's example, development of the family, the essence of the Holy Communion, and ultimately where our soul will spend eternity upon leaving this earth.

Our Sunday School teaching had similar overall objectives found within the universal Christian Church which is to learn about what and why one believes in the Christian faith. In the Catholic Church, this teaching is through the Catechism. It is a written work that explains the common beliefs of the Catholic faith as a teaching system. It is a list of questions and answers for Christians who practice the Catholic faith which helps believers to understand the essence of their belief.

I understand there are several catechisms beyond what I was learning in the Catholic Church as a young boy and in my youth. Each of these is used to teach within the Catholic universe, probably with particular meaningful variations: Anglican, Saint Pius X, Baltimore, Dutch, United States, and Filipino catechism. Learning about one's faith and practice is available for Catholics through the study of any of these Catechisms.

While the building facilities were limited in *Iglesia Bautista Del Salvador*, we offered four Sunday School classes. These were generally well attended. The Adults (*los Adultos*) gathered in the sanctuary surrounded by beautiful stained-glass lancet-styled windows on the first floor. The teacher was generally a man, and sometimes a woman, who taught the class in Spanish using the Bible as it basic text. They also used other related teaching handouts in Spanish. Teachers were adults chosen from this particular age group who came prepared spiritually and committed to earnestly review their lesson materials in order to teach effectively.

Their classes were interactive to produce the best meaning and understanding of the material being studied. I found this approach useful in expanding my Spanish speaking and reading and using it in our native language. It seemed that this class never had sufficient time to complete its session. At the conclusions they stayed where they were as the time transitioned into the morning general service.

The Youth (*los Jóvenes*) used either of two small rooms behind the pulpit. One was where I was a student and later taught the class. Each was minimally heated in winter or cooled in summer but enclosed by beautiful lancet-styled stained-glass windows as found in the sanctuary. Our class used a curriculum purchased from recognized Christian printing sources available: the Baptist Press, David C. Cook publishing company, and other sources.

After a while, the youth group elected me to teach this energetic group of ten of my cohorts who were mostly teenagers. Though I did not have her as a teacher, Martha López Marcano shared with me in early 2021, her memories about how her class use to meet in a tiny classroom in the basement near the entrance to the room. As we spoke, I sensed her enthusiasm in teaching youth about Christ many decades ago.

I had to prepare to teach well and I perused my Bible days before each class. I also studied materials such as books, maps and articles related to the lesson. I used interactive discussions suggested by the study guide and from the Sunday School Department superintendent. Our class discussed any of the thirty-nine Books of the Old Testament and God's work before Christ came to the world. We also studied the twenty-seven New Testament Books and about how we could apply the readings from both of these sources within our contemporary living and continuing spiritual development.

The Royal Ambassadors for Christ class was group composed of junior high school age youth. Their class met in the balcony with their teachers who conducted the class in English. As I did not associate frequently with this group, I cannot adequately comment about their activities. However, I remember that they were a lively and active group of youth who loved and followed the Lord and His ways. This group had many individuals who were recognized in several activities in this congregation and other Christian groups.

The youngest Sunday School class was the Children's group (Los Niños). It was usually led by a woman and a team of assistants from the congregation, including youth from the Junior High group. Some of their teachers are discussed elsewhere in this book. Because of their numbers, they needed adequate space in which to hold their class; therefore, they were assigned to the beautifully cedarwood paneled basement and occupied most of the three-thousand square feet available in this room.

The incandescent lighting in the room was enhanced by some six windows along the east and six on west sides of the room's high walls. These were often covered with translucent cloth curtains confected by the women's group. Heating and ventilating issues this room were perennial challenges throughout the seasons until these issues were partially ameliorated. The children sat in a circle on small chairs. The teachers used the Bible and other Christian teaching material bought from approved Christian sources and used their own enthusiastic ingenuity that was appropriate for the children's ages.

This class was generally taught in English as the children were English-speaking dominant Mexican Americans and some newcomers from other Latin American backgrounds. They were taught about stories based on Bible personalities and events, Christian living, and joyful singing. They discussed how the stories could be applied in their lives at home, in recreation, and the principal commandment that we are to love God, others, oneself and obey our parents. *Los Niños* class was a valuable source for youthful singers and actors for Christmas and Easter services which were celebrated in the sanctuary annually with the entire congregation.

When Sunday School ended at 10:30 a.m., all class groups quickly moved to the sanctuary if they were not already here. Various men or women served as Superintendent of Sunday School and led this part of the program. We sang choruses and had wrap-up activities: each class group or individuals would orally recite the "memory verse" which was the essence of the class lesson, paper sticky gold stars were awarded to the group or individual who had memorized the morning Bible verse; birthdays were announced followed by everyone singing "Happy Birthday" or *"Feliz, Feliz, Cumpleaños,"* which had a different melody.

After singing, a prayer was raised to God thanking Him for the time shared together, other praises, and remembering the sick. Visitors were also recognized at this time. The thirty-minutes wrap-up time flew by quickly. The younger children would recess to the basement for their own program activities or remain with their parents in the sanctuary for the morning worship service. All other adults and youth were invited to remain in the pews.

Sunday Morning Worship Services

Immediately after closing Sunday School, Sunday morning worship service[56] was celebrated from 11:00 a.m.-12:00 p.m., in the sanctuary. During the service, families sat together with their friends and invited guests. All who attended were encouraged to bring their Bible, though Spanish versions of these and hymnals were available in the racks behind each pew. The service began with an organ prelude. Upon finishing, a few notes lead everyone to stand and sing the *"Doxología* (Doxology),"* and sometimes, *"Gloria Demos al Padre* (Glory Be to the Father)," two historic pieces of Christian worship music.

The pastor would step to the lectern to raise a hearty prayer to God for: our health, the day, our jobs, the sick, our leaders, world peace, missionaries, followed by *"bienvenido"* (welcome) to everyone in attendance without anyone leaving their seats to circulate in the room to greet the other congregants.

A congregational hymn was sung followed by a reading from the Old or New Testament; or an antiphonal reading was selected from those found at the end of the hymnal and everyone was invited to orally read the designated passage in unison. Antiphonal readings filled the sanctuary with the voices of the worshippers in an uplifting manner confident that God heard them.

After the reading, the congregation would be requested to sit. If scheduled, the choir would sing a choral anthem, or another hymn was sung.

Holy Communion service would then be served by the deacons as described earlier in this text.

Thereafter, the pastor would deliver his sermon for the morning for forty-five or more minutes, in Spanish. It was often a continuation from the previous Sunday or the beginning of a new sermon series. At the close of his message, an *"invitación* (invitation)" was made to anyone to raise their hand or step forward if the person wished to receive Christ as their personal savior or become a member of this church. Transfer of membership to this church would follow the discussion presented earlier.

On scheduled dates, before the pastor's morning sermon, the dedication or presentation of babies and small children was celebrated. This was when the parents and friends would bring the child to the pulpit. This event was officiated by the pastor. He would hold the baby or young child for all to see and announce their name.

The pastor would ask the parents to vocally confirm their promise to God to raise the child in a Christian environment. Upon affirming, the pastor would raise a prayer imploring Christ and God to become an integral part of the child's life forever. The pastor would then turn to the congregation and have them promise to help the parents to fulfill their oath by expressing a vigorous, "sí."

Tithes and offerings were collected by the deacons either before or after the sermon or presentation of babies. A hymn was sung, and the pastor expressed a Christ-filled benediction on everyone. Before leaving for home, parents were reminded to gather their children who may have participated in the basement activities. A final organ postlude was played as the congregants exited the sanctuary.

Sunday Evening Services

In addition to Sunday morning worship services and the exciting Sunday School activities, two others were held in the evening. One was the youth Los Jóvenes who held their hourlong evening program in the basement. These were celebrated in English from 6 p.m.-7 p.m., where we sang songs, read scripture, listened to an invited guest speaker, or had one of our own youth bring a message. I delivered a few messages. It was an exciting hour of Christian fellowship by and for our youth.

Often times, local Baptist youth groups with whom we associated attended our meetings to share information about what they were doing in their own congregations. It was also a time when we shared information to attend future Baptist associations or conventions that year. Some of these events are described in this book. After Los Jóvenes service was finished, all were invited to attend the regular evening worship service[57] in the sanctuary upstairs and almost all stayed.

A second general Sunday worship service was celebrated from 7 p.m. to 9 p.m. in the sanctuary. A brief organ prelude was played. Upon ending, the pastor would step forward from the large oak chair located behind the pulpit's back wall to extend a welcome. He then raised an opening prayer or had a prearranged congregant seated on the pulpit or a pew to thank God for His blessings and to dedicate our service to Him. A preselected or requested hymn was sung and accompanied by organ or piano. Thereafter, a Bible or antiphonal reading was led by a deacon or an assistant, followed by a brief time for making announcements of coming events to which we were invited.

The beginning of the service was designated números especiales (special numbers.) These were not scheduled every Sunday evening. When they were, it was when the sanctuary was filled with the voices of anyone who wished to praise God. Some sang a solo or duet from the hymnal or read a poem they had written. Most participants were generally older people of both genders. I was pianist for this service. I generally never knew beforehand who was going to sing until given the title that night whereupon I managed to find the hymn or played the song by memory if I recognized the piece.

One of these singers was my mother, Carmen. She loved to praise God through using her untrained alto voice. Oftentimes, a few days before the Sunday night program, she would tell me that she was planning to sing a particular hymn at the next service. We would sit at the piano at her home to practice her selection several times, in the key in which she felt comfortable singing. When the particular Sunday evening arrived, she would walk to the side of the piano to announce the title of her song. I played her an introduction in the key signature we had practiced. Suddenly, she would panic and start singing in a higher or lower key.

I quickly modulated to the new one and we proceeded. With God's grace we generally finished well. I often wondered whether anyone in the audience recognized what had just transpired. These were precious and indelible moments. Her unexpected key change provided me with piano transposition skills which I use even today with other singers. Her eldest son, my oldest brother, Augustine, would sometimes accompany her in a duet and they did very well.

Other people perennially attended números especiales. One was *hermano* (brother) Aristeo and Catalina Bautista, long-time, humble and aged congregants who generally sat in the second pew at the back right side of the sanctuary. Aristeo was an untrained baritone singer who loved to praise God through music. He did well and I could sense his feeling of accomplishment in his gift to God whenever he sang.

Isaiah Bautista, one of the above couple's six children majored in classical piano at the Chicago Conservatory of Music. He came one evening and played an advanced étude on the Chickering grand piano. He was a teenager, thin, tall, and sported slightly long pitch-black hair tied in a ponytail. I remember he seemed to have fingers longer than anyone I knew including mine. These were critical in playing his piece. He consistently delivered excellent performances. When completed, he would always bow. His delivery left us with our mouths agape. I often thought we were fortunate to have Isaiah in our congregation. I never knew what became of him.

Venustiano Garza was a singer who enjoyed lifting his tenor voice to sing in Spanish. I recall his favorite song was the Simmonds hymn, "*Con Eco Vivo De Tu Voz* (Lord, Speak To Me That I May Speak)." He not only sang the lyrics, but he also lived them throughout his life. He moved away from this area in the 1960s.

Sister (*hermana*) Anita Sasso Fierro shared with us her coloratura soprano voice which lifted everyone's spirit as she sang sacred pieces. Additional information about Anita's work in this congregation is discussed in another part of this book. She died in 1995 and left us with wonderful memories of her effective and consistent work for Christ.

After each of them completed their musical presentations, no one in the audience would overtly demonstrate their appreciation; the sanctuary was totally silent. In later years, polite clapping became acceptable.

Another fine singer was Sister Sara Hernández Magaña. She was a semi-trained coloratura soprano who occasionally participated in these evening services and was active in many musical programs in other venues throughout her life. She was a brilliant, talented, and young teenager at Bowen High School in South Chicago during the 1950s when I was a student here. Sara was petite, yet her voice was beautiful and powerful.

I remember one of her many performances in the cavernous auditorium of Bowen High School during a student assembly. She sang in German "Der Holle Rach" ("Hell's Vengeance Boils in my Heart"), an aria from Mozart's opera, *The Magic Flute*. This piece[58] required Sara to sing this "face-paced menacingly grandiose rage aria" in D minor with text in complex meters. She was able to reach a vocal range to cover "two octaves, from F4 to F6 and a very high tessitura, A4 to C6" with finesse. She brought down the house that afternoon. In *Iglesia*

Bautista Del Salvador, she sang beautifully in our choir or solo pieces for many years.

It would have been an extraordinary musical delight if we had considered having Anita and Sara sing the beautiful soprano duet, "Song to the Moon," by Dvorak. It would have brought together our two outstanding homegrown sopranos with musical enjoyment. However, we probably would not have heard this aria, nor the duet performed during our congregation's special numbers, as it was considered secular and inappropriate in our Baptist congregation.

We were blessed to be their contemporaries and recognized the voices God gave them in the genres of classical and sacred Christian music. Sara earned a master's degree which prepared her for a long and exciting career in teaching music at the elementary school level in Los Alamitos, California where she lived with her two children and husband, David Magaña, for many years. Sara left us too early in 2012 at sixty-nine years of age.

Wednesday Evening Meetings

Bible study services were held three out of the four Wednesday evenings[59] per month. These were held to maintain active participation of members beyond those celebrated on Sunday. They encouraged parishioners to worship in-person if they had missed Sunday services due to employment or other reasons. They were celebrated from 7:00 p.m. to 9:00 p.m., in the sanctuary. Everyone was invited, though the majority of these were adult members and a few friends. Attendance was minimal but spirited. People brought their Bibles with them to study the Word.

Everyone sat together as families or individually and visitors sat with their guests. Announcements were made about forthcoming campus events, a hymn was sung accompanied by the piano, prayers were lifted to God thanking Him for blessing received and healing of our sick congregants. Thereafter our offerings were collected. The focus of the evening services were in-depth Bible studies led by the pastor or a member based on biblical passages from the Old or New Testament. Though attendance was minimal the fellowship people experienced was uplifting in all our services. People said they looked forward to attending these mid-week gatherings throughout the year.

One Wednesday evening per month was designated as a general business meeting. Reports were presented by the pastor, deacons, officers, and committee chairs. They brought information about administrative, financial, Sunday School, youth activities, Hispanic Baptist association and conventions, and housekeeping on the status of on-going or new projects such as those discussed in this book.

Additional Christian Education

Other Christian education programs[60] were regularly scheduled in *Iglesia Bautista Del Salvador*, during summer. This program was a youth oriented program called Vacation Bible School. It was offered for one week using the church facilities as needed. It was organized around a Christian theme and open to all youth, including outreach to the general community. Adult men, women, and older youth helped in teaching and learning sessions, singing, coordinating recreational games, setting-up the premises and serving lunch. I participated in a limited number of these activities.

Another summer program was also sponsored by South Chicago Neighborhood House in which our youth were involved. This was a week-long camping event that was held in Indiana State Dunes, Camp Tepee, and White Pidgeon Camp, Michigan. We were transported on a large yellow school bus. It seemed to lack shock absorbers and rattled our bones to and from our destinations. We had to open the windows in summer to survive the interior heat of the bus and had fun singing camp songs as we were shuttled slowly over neighborhood and rural streets in Illinois, Indiana, Michigan before many state superhighways or tollways existed. I have forgotten most of the names of the staff of this "house," and I will discuss a few of them later.

For some youth, attending camp was a first-time away from home. It was interesting to watch them develop self-confidence in themselves through the activities in which they participated. Several youth from *Iglesia Bautista Del Salvador* served as camper-advisors. These included Paul Gonsález, Issac Barreto, Nathaniel Manzo, Sara Hernández Magaña, Lydia "Lee" Armas, Albino Vásquez Jr, and a number of other young people who helped our efforts. Today, only Paul and I are the surviving octogenarians from this cohort.

Special Music Programs

My wife and I were members of *Iglesia Bautista Del Salvador* for some twenty years. We enjoyed serving in many of its activities. We especially enjoyed singing in our adult choir, though I mainly served as director and pianist. Membership ranged from ten to twenty-five and occasionally we invited other choristers. All of our members were volunteers, and most did not read music. Yet they eagerly and quickly learned their parts to *"make a joyful noise unto the Lord."*

Somewhere in the mid-1950s, a young man started participating in our services. He was already here by the time I began attending. His name was, Feland L. Meadows, commonly known as "Phil." I learned he was American born and raised here and in México. This explained why he was totally bilingual and bicultural in Spanish and English. He may have been the son of Baptist missionary parents. I remember he was single, well educated, Anglo-looking with blond hair, very tall, thin, and had a warm Christian personality.

I understand that Phil was a student at the University of Chicago in Hyde Park. I do not recall anyone asking about his major studies at this fine university. Some said he was enrolled in its Divinity School, which was founded under Baptist auspices. He brought his experience to our congregation using his tenor voice, conducting skills and piano ability. He is credited for establishing the choir[61] in this congregation during the 1950s and often led our singing in Spanish and English.

In later years, he earned a Ph.D. from U.C. Berkeley and became a distinguished educator. He dedicated much of his professional work with the Montessori early childhood teacher preparation and learning system. Dr. Phil dedicated his professional career in international and American universities. On August 26, 2017, he celebrated his ninetieth birthday (1927-) and continued to be actively involved in programs at Keenesaw State University in the Goizueta Foundation, in Keenesaw, Georgia. My several attempts to reach him in 2022 were unsuccessful.

Our choir presented various Christian cantatas over the years. We used English in special presentations on Palm Sunday, Good Friday, and Easter. English and Spanish were used in Thanksgiving, Christmas Eve, and New Year's Eve programs. The latter two started around 9 p.m., in the basement, with a robust ethnic dinner, followed by a brief worship service in the sanctuary. It ended at midnight when the nearby steel mill sounded its loud industrial air horn that was heard throughout the neighborhood at the stroke of 12:00 a.m. to welcome the New Year. Though it was dark and very cold outside when we exited the building after the latter two celebrations, it was a joyous time to go home to continue to celebrate the Mid-night Christmas Service (*Noche Buena*) or the beginning of the New Year (*Año Nuevo*) in a family setting.

As is generally seen in many congregations of all faiths during the above services, large numbers of people filled the sanctuary and our spirits were uplifted. However, many of them would not be seen at the following service nor at other services held throughout the rest of the year, sometimes until twelve months later. In trying to assess the efforts and effectiveness of our programs, after the events our leaders met to discuss how we might improve our mission and effort in the community to share the Good News of Christ. We would consider the lessons learned and apply these in our services throughout the year.

It was during the morning Thanksgiving Service of 1957 (*Servicio de Acción de Gracias*), when we first introduced and used our new hymnal. It replaced an earlier one that had been used for years. It was a dark blue[62] colored hard covered book with Gothic gold colored lettering, "*Himnos de la Vida Cristiana (Hymns of Christian Living),*" with the hymns and antiphonal readings printed in Spanish. These helped the congregants to maintain and strengthen the Spanish skills they already had and to expand and improve it for those who wished to do so as I did.

This hymnal provided me invaluable information in my search about this Mexican Baptist congregation. It serendipitously allowed me a starting point to learn the name it used in 1957 which was influenced by its ethnicity when it was founded in 1926 and how in later years, it was modified which I discuss in this book.

Inside of first page of each hymnal I found an embossed tri-circle logo. The outer circle states, *PRIMERA IGLESIA BAUTISTA MEXICANA, S. CHICAGO, ILL.* The second inner circle: *FIRST MEXICAN BAPTIST CHURCH, S. CHICAGO, ILL.* The center one says, *EL SALVADOR.* I am unaware and cannot confirm whether a new logo was ever redesigned and used beyond this one when the congregation changed its name.

Sometime in late 1963, I was asked by the church directors to seek a new hymnal to replace the one we were using. I examined several books from various sources. I presented my report and was authorized to order fifty[63] copies of "*El Himnario (The Hymnal),*" published by the Rodeheaver Company, in conjunction with the Council on Spanish American Work. We received them in January 1964. It was a maroon-colored hard covered text. The cost of this order was around two hundred dollars and was a gift to the congregation by Ramón and Mary Martínez. I still have a signed hymnal with their appreciation note to me for leading our music effort. They were a gracious couple.

"*El Himnario*" did not display a logo or other information about the congregation imprinted in it. As with the earlier hymnals, these were placed in the small book racks in back of the pews that held offering envelopes and information cards. Like the previous hymnal, this one facilitated singing four-part harmony in Spanish and was printed in easy-to-read notes for piano accompaniment.

The new book contained many traditional Christian hymns sung in English-speaking congregations throughout Chicago and the USA. Like

Facilitator in Establishing the First Mexican Baptist Church in South Chicago

the former hymnal, this one also provided compositions originally written in Spanish by Latin American composers and had seasonal antiphonal readings in Spanish which were printed in the back pages of each text.

Beyond the hymnals, Ramón and Mary donated some twenty-five long black robes with accompanying white silk stoles in appreciation of the adult choir's work. We wore these for several years in our Sunday morning services when the choir or the smaller *grupo coral* sang when a full choir was not available. We also used them in services at other churches. I have found no photographs of the full choir wearing these beautiful vestments. This happened because we forgot to assign someone to do it. However, I found a photograph which shows a few choir members wearing them.

Our congregation developed and maintained an exciting music program for decades. Our adult choir arduously volunteered to share our gift of music in our congregation and with many other churches whenever we were invited.

For many years, our choir performed challenging choral anthems in English and Spanish. For example, in Thanksgiving services, we sang Tannhauser's, "Pilgrims Chorus*,*" *and* O'Reilly/Dickon's*,* "Thanks Be to God (*Gracias a Dios.*)" During Christmas season, we sang selections from Handel's, "*Messiah*," or Théodore Duboise's cantata, "*The Seven Last Words of Christ,*" in English during our Good Friday services. It was Phil Meadows who introduced our choir to this level of sacred choral and congregational music as said above.

In addition to the above, our choir presented other majestic pieces in English and Spanish. These would include "The Holy City*,*" and "Onward Christian Soldiers (*Firmes y Adelante*)," by F.E. Weatherly and S. Adams, respectively. We also sang bilingually the powerful chorale as, Martin Luther's "A Mighty Fortress Is Our God (*Castillo Fuerte.*)"

My earliest exposure to choral music was while I studied at Bowen High School. It was located at 2710 E. 89th Street in South Chicago. For decades, it had an extraordinary music department when many *Iglesia Bautista Del Salvador* youth and I were students here.

Our teachers taught us challenging pieces written by a host of European composers such as Mozart, Brahms, Beethoven, Handel and others. I recall Mozart's gentle and serene "Motet in D major," "Ave Verum Corpus (Hail True Body)," a four-voice arrangement in Latin. Singing these beautiful sacred pieces did not raise anyone's concern about performing these in a public high school setting.

Because of the latter's beautiful music and theme, I introduced it to our choir, which we quickly learned. On one weekend in the 1960s we donned our choir robes and sang *"Ave Verum"* in Latin at a Spanish-speaking Baptist service in Hammond, Indiana where we were one of the several choirs that sang in the program. This piece was sung almost annually by the Bowen High School Mixed Choir in which I was a member and sang in for four years (1953-1957) under the direction of several accomplished music teachers.

During these high school years, I sang under the baton of two music faculty members: Mr. Clayton Fox, of Swedish background who looked physically like President Abraham Lincoln, and the bespeckled, balding, mustached man, Mr. Richard Widman, also of Swedish background who replaced Mr. Fox who transferred from this campus to another one during my junior year. We learned two wonderful pieces by Leroy Anderson: "Bugler's Holiday," an upbeat, rhythmic, toe tapping piece for three trumpeters, and "A Trumpeters Lullaby," a moderate piece for one trumpet, which Mr. Anderson wrote in 1954 for his friend and famous musician, Arthur Fiedler.

Other music faculty were Mrs. Mildred Caldwell, department chair, Mrs. Lillian Pope, and Mrs. Irene Collins. All of these teachers demonstrated a love for students and dared to bring challenging pieces to our working-class high school students. Female students could also enroll in the all-girls Treble Choir, under the direction of Mrs. Collins. Their concerts were college-level presentations.

A piece written for female voices and directed by Mrs. Collins was "Lift Thine Eyes," from Mendelssohn's sacred oratorio, *"Elijah."* Its lyrics are based on the Old Testament Books of I and II Kings and sung as an andante trio: "Lift thine eyes, O lift thine eyes, to the mountains, when cometh help. Thy help cometh from the Lord, the Maker of Heaven and earth. He has said, thy foot shall not be moved. The Keeper will never slumber." This text is also found in the Old Testament Book of Psalms, 121.

Interestingly, a Spanish version of this same text was sung frequently by men and women soloists in our Baptist evening services, "Alzaré Mis Ojos A Los Montes." It used a different melody and meter and though I never found music to it, I learned and played it on various occasions for a few soloists who sang it during números especiales discussed above.

Mrs. Caldwell also led classes in concert band, a full orchestra with a harp, and other small ensembles. Her name conjures memories of when she introduced us to new composers and their music.

In addition to the youth of *Iglesia Bautista Del Salvador* being involved in the above high school's fine arts programs some participated in Bowen High School's athletic activities. I admired Daniel M. López, who did very well in wrestling. Sara Hernández Magaña and Anna López Jiménez were recognized for their participation in women's athletics. All three earned many awards for their outstanding athletic prowess and abilities and brought collective pride to our congregation's youth.

A Good Friday Cantata

Since the 1950s and many years thereafter, *Iglesia Bautista Del Salvador's* choir and congregation came together on Good Fridays[64] to commemorate the crucifixion of Jesus Crist and its significance to the overarching history of our Savior. I especially remember two of these historic events.

One program was celebrated on Good Friday, March 27, 1964, at 7:30 p.m., Chicago time. Rev. Eugenio Hanchuck was our pastor. He began the service with a prayer, made some introductory remarks about the meaning of the service, thanked the choir for their effort in presenting this cantata, and expressed a warm welcome to the members of the congregation and invited guests.

The adult choir sat on the sanctuary pulpit in the newly hewn home-made plywood raisers which I designed and assembled so the singers had an unobstructed view of the director, organist and pianist, and could be seen clearly by the audience.

They sat in the typical four-voice section arrangement facing the congregation. Each singer was donned in a black choir robe with a white silk stole and was prepared to worship and praise God through the music we had rehearsed extensively on Thursday nights for several months before this event.

Everyone came that evening to hear the beautiful music of the oratorio written by the prolific French choirmaster, composer and organist, Théodore Dubois, *The Seven Last Words*[65] *of Christ*. It was first performed in France in 1867, under the title, *Les Sept Paroles du Christ*. Here we were, ninety-seven years later, performing this sacred choral music in South Chicago. In 2023, this music is rarely heard.

This oratorio used Christ's last words as He was dying on the cross on Mt. Calvary (Golgotha) after being crucified that Friday between 9:00 a.m. and 3:00 p.m. in Jerusalem, Israel. Each piece is based on His words as found in the Gospels of Matthew, Mark, Luke, and John.

Dubois used Christ's memorable expressions from these texts to write a beautiful oratorio in a choral setting that revealed His sorrowful words. This composition was originally written for organ only accompaniment to support the chorus, including solos singing each *Word*.

The oratorio begins with the "Introduction," sung by a soprano solo (Anita Sasso Fierro), who delivers a short lament, "O all ye who travel upon the highway, harken to me, and behold me; was e'er sorrow like unto my sorrow? For the Lord Almighty has dealt bitterly with me. Call me now no more Naomi, from today call me Mara."

The "First Word," was sung by a baritone (Peter Béloz), tenor Lee Armas, and choir, "Father, forgive them, for they know not what they do."

The "Second Word," a duet, was sung by a tenor and baritone, with choir: "Verily, thou shalt be in Paradise today with me. Amen, so I tell thee."

The "Third Word," was sung by soprano, tenor, baritone soloists, with the choir: "See, O Woman!" with the moving verse, "Here behold thy Son beloved. See your mother, bow'd in anguish, who beside the cross doth languish, where on high her son is borne. Is there mortal, who not feeleth to behold her where she kneeleth, so woeful, and so forlorn?"

The "Fourth Word," was a baritone solo, "God, my Father, why hast Thou forsaken me?"

The "Fifth Word," was sung by the choir, tenor, and baritone soloists, "I am athirst!"

The "Sixth Word," "Father, into Thy hands I commend my soul," was sung by the tenor solo and choir.

The "Seventh Word," "It is finished!" was sung by soprano, tenor and baritone soloists, and choir.

When the choir sings the final word and comes to the phrase "...all the rocks were rent, and all the graves were open'd wide," it ceases singing, and the organ transitions from an andante maestoso voicing into four different ones.

Each new voicing becomes slightly stronger until it reaches the full sound of the organ (tutti) for thirty bars with parts of these in a minor key, as the organ attempts to capture the pain Christ was suffering as His life departs His body on the cruel cross. Upon reaching the end of this part, the tempo slows significantly until the music becomes softer with a much slower tempo.

As the music diminishes, a short somber "Prayer" is interwoven within the score to beautifully complete the oratorio. It took over an hour to perform. We sang in English. Other choirs have sung it in its original language, French, and others have performed it in Latin and Spanish.

The second part of this narrative describes the anxiety that was occurring in the sanctuary as the choir was singing the beautiful "Fifth Word." Suddenly, the whole building began to quake. It was definitely an event that frightened everyone as they sat in the sanctuary and listened. What we were experiencing was a 9.2 temblor that erupted in Prince William Sound in Anchorage, Alaska around 5:36 p.m. PM AKST.

It lasted four minutes and thirty-eight seconds and though thousands of miles northwest of South Chicago, the building here quaked noticeably as if we were close to the epicenter. The next day, March 28, 1964, the *Chicago Tribune* reported the "Alaska Quake Disaster."[66]

I continued to play the organ and looked at the hanging ceiling lights as they slightly swayed back and forth and could hear the creaking of the seventy-nine-year-old building as the quake rolled through the area. I was very concerned that the light fixtures might snap from their mounts.

I looked and saw expressions of concern on people's faces and saw their fear. I maintained a settled appearance confident that God was in control of this natural event. As I continued to play, I was thinking to myself what we would do if the structure began to collapse.

The temblor magnitude was definitely weaker and less destructive than what was experienced in Anchorage. However, it was frightening for everyone who was present that evening. The choir continued to sing but I feared we might have to stop and evacuate the building if the situation continued or followed by an aftershock. Neither happened. We were able to complete the cantata in just over an hour.

Pastor Hanchuk came to the pulpit and expressed thanks to the choir, shared some assuring words, lifted a prayer to God to remind us of the essence of this service and the event we experienced and dismissed us. The room was quiet as we all withdrew. A few choristers remained to listen to the tape recording we made of the program and could hear the distortion on it as the quake passed through. I do not know what became of this recording.

The oratorio presentation was possible through God's support and dedicated choristers who wished to celebrate this part of our Christian history through sacred music. They were, Adela Gonsález, Ruth Rivera Béloz, my wife, Alice Báez, Ernestina Barreto, Angeline De Hoyos, Anita Sasso Fierro, Eunice Fierro Robles, Silvia (Timmy) Garza, Mary Martínez, Lydia "Lee" Armas, Anita Armas Estéviz, Larry Autry, Peter Béloz, and other singers. Though most of these choristers are deceased today the memory of this service and the temblor are indelible.

Other Choir Programs

On Good Friday, April 16, 1965, again, our choir brought another musical program[67] to our congregation. It was basically comprised of the same singers, including soloists from the 1964 program. Rev. Humberto Salinas was the pastor this year. He had recently succeeded Pastor Hanchuk.

We came together to sing this cantata titled, *The Story of Easter,* a composition for five voices, by Ellen Jane Lorenz. It is comprised of twenty-four short pieces for male and female soloists, duets, and choir in combination with congregational hymns in which the audience participated nine times throughout the program. The lyrics for the fourteen hymns, various solos, and choir pieces are derived from selected verses of the New Testament Book of St. Matthew: 16, 20-21, and 26-28.

The cantata begins with a Baritone voice recitative and choir of "Take Up Thy Cross," and ends with the audience joining the choir to sing, "Easter Benediction," and "Fling Out the Banner." The entire program lasted about an hour. Interestingly, a printed note at the end of the program announced:

"A free will offering will be collected at the end of the program. This offering will be set aside and used for the 'lot fund' for the purchase of land adjacent to our building."

This note relates to the successful purchase of three parcels of land discussed above.

We recorded this program and have it in my files. In late fall of 2021, I went to the home of Dr. Theresa Mosqueda and Rudy Ponce who had a vintage reel-to-reel Akai tape recorder where I was able to hear the choral music as it was performed fifty-six years earlier. It was a real joy to hear it again.

Our congregation members and adult choir also participated in two other annual Chicago-wide *"servicios unidos"* (united services). One was celebrated on Thanksgiving Day (Día de Acción de Gracias) November 27, 1958, on the campus of the First Congregation Church (*Primera Iglesia Congregacional*) located at 110 N. Ashland Avenue.

This program was organized by *La Asociación Ministerial Hispana* (Hispanic Ministerial Association) and represented twenty Spanish-speaking organizations and congregations who attended that early morning: eight Baptists, one Congregational, two Mennonite, two Methodist, one Pentecostal, one United Brethren, one Salvation Army, one Christian, one Evangelical, one Biblical Center, and one Spanish-speaking radio station in Cicero, Illinois. This event reflected the increasing Evangelical Spanish-speaking ministry that was actively growing in those years.

The theme of this service was based on Psalm 92, verse 1, "*Es bueno dar gracias a Dios* (It is good to give thanks to God)," as expressed on the cover of the program.

The program began with fifteen minutes of majestic pipe organ music. The organist was Mr. George Rico, a prolific music teacher in the Chicago Public School system. He played Bach's "Toccata and Fugue in D Minor," and two other Bach compositions, "Andante," and, "Revene." He also played sweeping organ adaptions of traditional hymns: Briggs,' "*O Que Amigo Nos Es Cristo* (What a Friend We Have in Jesus)," *"Firmes Y Adelante"* of Baring-Gould's, "Onward, Christian Soldiers."

The service included other choral pieces and hymns in Spanish and English directed by Angelo Rico, George's brother. Our adult choir combined our voices in several choral anthems along with those of several other choirs. We sang: *"A Ti, Oh Dios* (To Thee, O God)," The Heavens Are Telling, *"Te Adora Toda Lengua* (All Tongues Adore Thee)," *"Salmo 150 (*Psalm 150*),"* and, *"Dios Te Bendiga Y Te Guarde* (God Bless and Keep You)."

A children's choir representing the music institute of the area's social service agency Casa Central brought some beautiful choral pieces as they sang alongside the adult choir seated in the horse shoe shaped balcony high above the sanctuary floor. They appeared and sounded angelic.

The guest speaker was Rev. F. Soto Fontáñez, pastor of *Iglesia Bautista de Brooklyn, New York*, a powerful messenger of the Gospel and Christian leader who was active over many years in the Spanish-speaking Baptist ministry. It is historical to note that *Iglesia Bautista Del Salvador* was listed under its earlier name, *Iglesia Bautista 'El Salvador'* with Rev. Pedro Cruz as pastor.

The names of the nineteen pastors for each of the congregations are indicated, including one radio station sans the director's name. The officers for *La Asociación Ministerial Hispana* were being installed in this service: president, Rev. L. Aréyzaga; secretary, Mario O. Snyder; treasurer, Samuel Smith, and Ariel Curet as director. For many years, these pastors, and the other members of this *Asociación* were active in this group. Each used their talents to unite these congregations in such beautiful and meaningful annual services to the glory of God.

Our choristers departed South Chicago early in the morning in private autos in order to arrive on time at this early morning Thanksgiving service. Here we joined many choir members and other guests who were representing the above congregations. In spite of the many people that attended, we barely filled the cavernous sanctuary of the church. Nonetheless, we knew it was going to be a spirit-filled service.

The theme for a second united Thanksgiving service was, "*Bendice Alma Mía a Jehová y No Olvides Ninguno De Sus Beneficios,*" *Salmo 103:2* (Bless The Lord O My Soul and Forget Not All His Benefits)" from Psalm 103, verse 2. It was celebrated early morning on Thursday, November 24, 1959, in the same sanctuary listed above on the northwest side of Chicago. Again, it was organized by the *Asociación Ministerial Hispana*.

The Baptists churches alone composed fifty percent of the twenty organizations. Pastor Pedro Cruz, continued as our minister and the congregation's name is shown as *"El Salvador."* Again, we met Mr. George Rico as he played Bach's great pipe organ piece, "Toccata and Fugue in D Minor." The sermon was based on the above biblical reference. The message was brought to us by Rev. Lester T. Hersey, Mennonite pastor and director of the radio program in Puerto Rico, "Luz Y Verdad (Light and Truth.)"

These united services were a meaningful development of our Christian life in *Iglesia Bautista Del Salvador*. Through them we learned what the other Evangelical and Baptist congregations were doing in music and their work to spread the Gospel throughout various Hispanic neighborhoods in Chicago and parts of Indiana.

The groups were led by dozens of Christian men and women of all ages who were our mentors and outstanding role models. Though many of these early leaders have transitioned from this earth, the memory of their words and deeds still resonate in our minds.

Children in Music and Dramas

Iglesia Bautista Del Salvador had children's choirs[68] and exciting dramas in which they participated. These were celebrated during Easter, Thanksgiving and Christmas. Many of them participated in singing and oral recitations in Spanish and English which touched everyone's heart. Their directors were parents from our congregation who loved to serve the Lord. Children's participation was important to bring them into our services early in their lives where they were recognized for their individual and group effort which strengthened their understanding of Christ through music and words.

Their parents dressed each of them in beautiful children's outfits; sometimes they wore stoles that were sown by their mothers and worn over their clothes. As usual, the children looked angelic as they performed in our programs.

When they were scheduled to be present, their parents brought them punctually to rehearsals and performances. The children were always ready and eager to sing a solo, in a group or to recite individual lines. Raúl Pérez, son of Elisa and Frank Pérez, shared with me a beautiful anecdote about how he and Benjamín Salinas, the oldest son of pastor Humberto and Socorro Salinas, would compete with one another hoping to be selected for a singing part in the children's choir.

The children's enthusiasm brought quiet sighs of joy to the parent for their child and the group's overall effort during a morning or an evening service. As the children grew and matured, some transitioned into junior choir. In later years a few became members of our adult choir and acted in Christian plays as well.

Work with our older Youth was also exciting and full of many activities that would encourage them to participate in religious and other programs. One group was called, Royal Ambassadors for Christ, which many other congregations also had. It was designed specifically for them to have wholesome fun on one hand, while simultaneously providing them a solid Christian foundation for living Christ-filled lives at school, home, with friends or wherever they were.

This program encouraged youth to invite friends from school and the neighborhood to their programs. Several caring adults supervised their events. As I was too old to participate in this group, my direct experience in and recollection of their events is limited.

Beauty in Historic Houses of God

To celebrate the 1958 and 1959 Thanksgiving services we met in the historic almost century-old house of God[69] built in 1869-1871. It was the Union Park Congregational Church, next to the equally historic Carpenter Chapel, 60 N. Ashland Boulevard, on Chicago's Near West Side. The former was designed in the Gothic Revival-architectural design. Today, it is known as the First Baptist Congregational Church located on West Washington Boulevard.

As said earlier, since we arrived early on each occasion, we had the opportunity to admire the exterior and interior of the building. Most of our time indoors was spent in the sanctuary. We were in awe at the expansive pulpit and large communion table placed at its center and the other artifacts in this room.

On both occasions, we observed the immense size of the many stained-glass windows. These were in great contrast to the ones in our steel-making community's *Iglesia Bautista Del Salvador* or those installed by the First Baptist Church of South Chicago.

We saw the magnificent beauty and the enormous size and design of the sanctuary's two-story lancet and lite-tracing stained-glass windows. The windows of the north and south transepts and the east and south rose windows of the sanctuary amazed everyone. As we looked at these and size of the building, some choristers commented it reminded them of Saint Michael Archangel Roman Catholic Church, located in the *Bush*, a neighborhood close to our home congregation. I had to agree with them.

Union Park Congregational Church and St. Michael's Archangel Roman Catholic Church buildings are magnificent in their architectural beauty and size. Each used a variation of the Gothic Revival design. The first church was begun in 1869 and constructed totally of beige Lemont, Illinois sandstone and wood, thirty-eight years before the cornerstone of the latter was placed in 1907 and opened in 1909. This latter edifice used brown brick, steel, and sandstone on its exterior infrastructure. The local U.S. Steel Company donated the steel that was used to build it to thank and honor the Polish Americans who worked for this nascent steel company and were ninety percent[70] of the communicants in this church. Both buildings are extant in 2024.

We also learned of their contrasting community histories. The Union Park Congregational Church we see today is the second building for this congregation. It was built mostly by wealthy Scotch and Irish immigrant families of this early Chicago community soon after the Civil War. On the other hand, Saint Michael Archangel Roman Catholic Church was founded by poor working class Polish immigrant families who lived in South Chicago. Both structures are magnificent pieces of architecture that remind us of man's effort to soar the heights above their local streets in their efforts to reach and glorify God.

I remember how anxious we were to start our morning rehearsals in Union Park Congregational Church. During the service we heard the beautiful voices of over one-hundred adults and a children's choir as we sat in the oval amphitheater-style seating. The choirs were seated above the audience in the beautiful, curved balcony and historic sanctuary surrounded by huge wood carved ceiling beams. We were overwhelmed by the overall beauty of this masterfully constructed and designed building.

I subsequently learned that it and the adjacent Carpenter Chapel, which we only saw from the exterior, were built from the same Lemont sandstone. Both were listed on the National Register of Historical places in 2006. In the past, I thought the old Baptist building in South Chicago might receive recognition as did the two Congregational buildings. This is doubtful since major structural modifications have been made to the building e.g., extension of the original structure, removal of the lancet windows and its tower, and other significant structural modifications made over the decades.

I recall that as we sang in the choir loft of this over a century-old building the wood floor would vibrate whenever Mr. Rico played certain bass notes on the giant pipe organ. It made me reflect on the strength of this structure which was barely touched by the two-day Great Chicago Fire of October 1871 that destroyed hundreds of other

Chicago homes and churches. The building was constructed when South Chicago was an undeveloped immigrant community in Ainsworth until 1889 when it became a part of Chicago.

I was in awe at the size of Union Park Congregational Church's pipe organ and its beautiful overall design. I knew that we were about to hear a huge contrast between our simple two-manual Hammond organ in South Chicago and this one.

To get an historical background of this organ, I learned that a wealthy family in their congregation had contributed thousands of dollars to replace an earlier one. This anecdote contrasts greatly with how the *Iglesia Bautista Del Salvador* congregants had to schedule fundraisers to make and sell tamales and celebrated other events to pay for the cost of the small Hammond electronic organ during the early 1950s.

I found a picture of the Congregational church's sanctuary which displayed this huge bronze-colored organ. It had hundreds of pipes of various lengths and widths mounted onto the instrument's curved façade. It could be the W.W. Kimble organ that was newly installed or updated during the mid-1950s when our choir sang here. It offers numerous features from which to choose to produce powerful sounds: four manuals, 5,466 pipes (observable and unseen), seven divisions, seventy-four stops, and other advanced pipe organ amenities which have been continuously installed to over the years.

I never attended a mass in St. Michael Archangel Roman Catholic Church, but as a child, I walked past this Neo-Gothic style building for four years on my way to the original William K. Sullivan Elementary School when I lived in the *Bush* neighborhood. One Saturday morning as I was peddling by on my bicycle, I heard beautiful music coming from the organ which I did not see. I later learned it was a Möeller organ.

It was considered one of the fifteen finest *Grand Era* instruments in Chicago. Its music uplifted ones spirit during Catholic masses and wedding heard in Polish, English, and Spanish. In 2021, after over 112

Facilitator in Establishing the First Mexican Baptist Church in South Chicago

years, the building was closed and parishioners were directed to another parish.

Today, the organ, hundreds of square feet of stained glass and lineal feet of precious wood as butternut, Birdseye Maplewood and rare oak are extant throughout the interior of the building. A Steinway concert grand piano covertly brought into Music Hall of the 1893 World's Colombian Exposition's in Chicago to be played by Polish virtuoso pianist, composer and later statesman, Ignace Jan Paderewski, also remains in the building. Unless it receives Chicago Landmark historic status, its future and contents are minimally secure. I am sure the best decision will be made by the entrusted Church and community leaders.

Side view, Saint Michael Archangel Roman Catholic Church in the *Bush* community, looking south easterly. It is located at 8237 S. South Shore Drive, Chicago, Illinois. This Gothic styled church opened in 1909 to serve a predominantly Polish immigrant community. The steel used to construct it came from the local steel mills just five streets to the east. The building had a capacity of seating 2,000 people. Before it closed in October 2021, the last largest ethnic groups in it were Polish and Spanish- speaking parishioners, The structure is extant in 2024. (Source: G. Béloz, 2017.)

Another Thanksgiving United Service in which our adult choir participated was the one held on November 25, 1971, at 7 p.m. and hosted by the *Iglesia Bautista de Gary*, Indiana. We joined three other Baptist congregations at this service: *Segunda Iglesia Bautista de East*

Chicago, Indiana, *Iglesia Bautista de Sur Chicago,* and *Iglesia Bautista de Indiana Harbor,* Indiana.

The main speaker was the tireless pastor, Rev. Efraín Balderas, the well-recognized servant of God and an early pastor in our *Iglesia Bautista Del Salvador*. He occasionally donned a black robe when he preached but I cannot recall if he wore it that evening. He said this was attributed to his earlier Methodist ministry. The printed program does not provide information as to the names of the choirs that sang nor the hymns that were sung, but I am sure it was a joyous service filled with the spirit of God and fellowship.

As discussed at the beginning of this book, the congregation of First Baptist Church of South Chicago served God here for seventy-one years (1879-1950) as it brought the Gospel to this community in English. In the early 20th century, it had the opportunity to partner and plant a seed of a nascent group of Mexican emigrants and immigrants neighbors who sought to hear the *Good News* in Spanish.

My narrative provides valuable information[71] about their pastors and congregants and their histories as testaments of how each began to help spread the gospel of Jesus Christ throughout South Chicago and in other states via Baptist services, radio, education, conventions, associations and personal outreach.

Undoubtedly, God's grace and providence sustained these Baptist congregations collectively and as individual institutions throughout their long journeys, always being accompanied by and living and working within the Spirit of Christ.

This document also provides historic information about when and how the bilingual English and Spanish Community Christian Church of Chicago was founded.

PART IV:
LEADERSHIP AND DEVELOPMENT

Mexican Immigrants Choose South Chicago

In the early 19th century various peoples from Europe and the United States emigrated to the South Chicago area[72]. These include men, women, and children who represented German, Irish, English, Welsh, Swedish, Polish, Jews, French, Lithuanian, Greek, Croation, Serbian, Romanian, African, African American, and Mexican people. Each group or individual came to improve their living. Most arrived with entry labor skills and low formal education. They experienced hard, long workdays in their homelands and struggled to survive. Most brought little material wealth on their long journey here. Mexicans arrived in the mid-20th century and had a traceable history of having survived a diaspora similar to other immigrants who came to this community.

In South Chicago, each group's presence was fundamental to the overall growth and success[73] of new industries and opportunities that burgeoned around them. Their sweat equity increased industrial production and wealth for the corporation giants and investors in sales and services channels. Immigrant men worked on constructing houses, bridges, loading and off-loading boats, draining rivers and swamps, deburring iron and making steel products, shoveling tons of iron ore, manganese, and other minerals into dangerous hot giant steel-making blast furnaces, welding, and in myriads of jobs within the industries in and around the South Chicago area. Some started small businesses here similar to what they did in their homelands.

I knew and saw many Hispanic and other ethnic women who spent long hours dedicated to their family. They focused on muti-tasking and were the first-line health care providers, educators, cooks, counselors and were totally sage and always caring women. They were mentally and physically strong women who loved to serve in this and other churches and society groups in the community. Our Hispanic women were influenced and learned from other women they saw in public places as streets, stores, food markets, parks, movie houses, and in the denominational associations and conventions as discussed in this book.

As we know, it generally took another generation for most of these Hispanic and other women to advance as they received the opportunity to enter general and higher education and specialized training programs that led to better employment opportunities or careers. I saw such changes when Lee Armas, and Mary and Theresa Martinez entered and graduated as registered nurses. I also saw this change in Anita Sasso Fierro and Susie Apolinar Wells, our homegrown youth who were both college graduates in evangelical missionary studies as discussed here.

Mexicans who came to Chicago and South Chicago wished to live the American dream. They heard about and wanted to participate in the opportunities which many else were enjoying. Similarly, they came to fulfill their spiritual dreams of worshipping the God of their beliefs in Spanish in a Roman Catholic Church or Protestant denominations that were reaching out to this language group, especially by the Baptist leaders.

Written documentation has increased about the history of the early Mexicans who immigrated to Chicago. The narrative provides us with a clearer understanding of their one-hundred-five-year history of difficult struggles and marked success. We have data that details information about their arrival here, where and how lived, worked, and worshipped. To acquire information about these people, I perused an early study by Kerr: *Chicano Settlements in Chicago: Brief History*. While her work is very valuable, I used a recent research study by Michael Innis-Jiménez, *Steel Barrio: The Great Mexican Migration to South Chicago, 1915-1940*. This study provides detailed information about this ethnic group who came to this part of this community.

The latter refers to several earlier studies of this population and of how they lived in their adopted land. Mexicans travelled thousands of miles from their *patria* to come and settle in Chicago and then migrated to South Chicago in the early twentieth century. Several factors[74] caused "Tens of thousands, perhaps hundreds of thousands" to flee Mexico due to economic conditions, the 1910 Mexican Revolution, and religious persecution which caused them to come to the United States. Some dreamed to return but many never did.

Innis-Jiménez' research[75] indicates that in 1916, the first Mexican immigrants arrived in the South Chicago area. They were recruited to work in the railroad industry. Illinois Central railroad company was principally brought to Chicago by Senator Stephen Douglas in the early 1850s and it continued to grow in the 20th century. Mexican workers who were hired by the big railroad companies were known as "*traqueros* (trackworkers)." The railroad companies also hired other men called "*enganchistas* (labor agents)," to seek and recruit Mexican migrants for work in the railroad companies in entry-level jobs in various states and in the Chicago area.

It created a tripartite symbiotic relationship which benefited the migrants, enganchistas, and the employment needs of some nine major railroad companies that operated in and out of this local area for decades. The Mexicans derived[76] from the U.S. Southwest, Texas, Kansas and Missouri, says Innis-Jiménez. In time, they came from other closer states and cities in the Midwest as well.

Another major factor which attracted the Mexican immigrants to come to this state, city and community in 1917 was the involvement of the U.S. in World War I. When American men were conscripted into military service, levels of economic and industrial production began to fall in the areas of steel output, shipping, and in the railroad industry. Here in the South Chicago area, all of these sectors clamored for workers to maintain their revenue.

Similarly, the impetus for Mexicans to come to Chicago and South Chicago was an event that occurred September 22, 1919. Steelmaking was the king of industry as cotton production was in the South. It was faced with a strike[77] of 365,000 workers in fifty cities and ten states. This event, and another major social-racial eruption in Chicago on July

The First Baptist Church of South Chicago

27, shortly before the strike began brought an ugly and deadly riot against the African Americans living in the area.

The negative impact on Carnegie/South Works workers in South Chicago was significant. Additional workers had to be brought in to replace the strikers. Corporate officers in railroad and steel making companies considered racial preferences to replace the workers they were losing. To meet steel-production contracts and labor shortage during 1916-1920s, Mexicans were brought to South Chicago to work.

The steel-making bosses determined that Mexicans were the preferred workers in this situation and their recruitment commenced vigorously. Now began their history of becoming employees of the giant steel making industry, long after the thousands of Europeans who principally helped build it on the sandy shores of Lake Michigan. As the men entered the strike lines barriers, they were unaware of the meaning of words "scab" and "strike breaker," and endured a host of derogatory four-letter words in English and other languages. Still, they continued to report for work while fearing for their lives. In time, their lives improved meagerly in employment, housing, health, education, and freedom of religion in spite of the myriad social barriers they experienced for decades.

Immigrants were not strangers to tough work. They had already experienced it in their home country: onerous. They sought to be given a chance to work, and they would prove themselves worthy in spite of their limitations in English language and job skills. They had to quickly learn a new vocabulary. They used novel words in Spanish which were derived from English, and often called "Spanglish," e.g., train (*el tren*), railroad track (*el traque*), push (*puchar*), paycheck (*el cheque de pago*), rent (*la renta*), strike (*el estryk*), car brakes (*las brecas*), lunch (*el lonche*), in their expanding vocabulary. We heard such words throughout the neighborhood by Spanish-speaking workers, relatives and friends.

The early Mexicans railroad workers in this community lived in converted railroad cars provided by the railroad companies. These were located in the poorest part of South Chicago and provided limited hygienic living conditions for years. I never saw the railroad car sites as they may have been razed before I knew about them, and I did not know anyone who lived in them. Recent documentaries describe how they lived and suffered for years in these conditions. Here they lived and raised their children. Single male workers lived in boxcars apart from those designated for families.

Two other important factors[78] brought Mexican immigrants to Chicago and South Chicago. One was the *Cristero War*, the *Cristero Rebellion*, or *La Cristiada* struggle which throughout Mexico during 1924-1929. It was a reaction by the Mexicans and the Catholic Church leaders who interpreted the Articles of the Mexican Constitution of 1917 as being oppressive to the citizens and violently anti-Catholic. This period was very disruptive and destructive to the entire country and its population. People determined to flee Mexico and the Mexican diaspora was launched similar to what the Jewish people experienced during the 1930s-1940s, sans the atrocities that the latter group suffered during this decade and longer.

Another serendipitous factor[79] that brought Mexican nationals and emigrants to Chicago, South Chicago, and other states was the U.S. immigration law which caused "increased labor shortages in the industrial Midwest." As Mexicans were "exempt from the 1921 and 1924 quota laws, they became by default the choice for employers who did not want to hire African Americans." Mexican families were appearing throughout streets and neighborhoods of South Chicago along with all the other earlier immigrant groups.

These new residents were driven by various forces to participate in employment opportunities all around them. Their inner confidence and economic need helped to survive employment discrimination by employers and other immigrant groups who arrived in the area before them. In 1910 the number of Mexicans in Chicago[80] were 440; 1920: 1,141; 1930: 19,632, and in 1940 their numbers fell to 16,000. These data provide us a perspective as we recall that the *Iglesia Bautista Del Salvador* began in 1926 with a small congregation within the building of the First Baptist Church of South Chicago.

Innis-Jiménez states that in 1925, in a survey sponsored by the City of Chicago, discovered more than fifty percent[81] of the heads of household stated they hailed principally from three Central Mexican states: Guanajuato, Jalisco, and Michoacán. By 1936, this Mexican tri-state representation in South Chicago alone had grown to sixty-three percent of the residents.

Upon arriving in the area their *compatriotas* (compatriots), who were already living here may have written them to come and find each other in the community. This linkage helped families to fulfil their needs for stability and comfort in their new environment. They could reminisce about their homeland to help them sustain their culture, language and customs. They compared their new experiences and discussed job opportunities in the numerous industries in South Chicago that urgently needed workers.

They experienced overt and subtle discrimination in parts of South Chicago. They were often viewed as being foreign-born nuisances and being less than people. I remember hearing such expressions in public venues. I thought this was like the pot calling the kettle black when many of the critics experienced the same overall living and working condition when they arrived here as immigrants just a few years earlier. It was amazing how quickly many of our neighbors forgot the struggles they faced on the way to becoming Americans.

Mexican families often experienced housing discrimination when they sought to rent or buy homes throughout South Chicago. They endured the pejorative experiences through personal and collective strength, family ties, support from friends in local organizations, teachers in school, and their Christian education and personal faith.

While most of the Mexican immigrants remained Roman Catholic, I, and part if my family converted to the Protestant faith. When I began to attend *Iglesia Bautista Del Salvador* as a teenager, I learned many congregants had similar backgrounds before becoming Baptists. I also saw that some of the members and their families had progressed to various levels of economic success.

While the majority of families rented in houses having two or three flats, a few were able to purchase wood frame, single and multi-family units. Those who owned multi-flat structures augmented their income by renting the unused units to Mexican or other families. They were proud of their successful status in life. They were good neighbors by helping their ethnic *gente* (people). I knew several families in our congregation who had reached this level of economic growth.

None of the buildings had whole-house heating. Generally, the residences were heated by potbelly or a variety of iron stoves called heaters. Some of these had fancy enameled covers to protect anyone who accidentally touched them, especially families with children. Stoves were centrally located in the middle room with the flue from it protruding to the nearest chimney. The rooms farthest from the stove received the least warmth. During the winter months, the stoves were hand-fired with coal, coke, wood, card board, and newspapers. Local railroad companies discarded railroad ties in various empty lots where neighbors could haul them away, saw to size and use them for fuel. As these were commercially presoaked in creosote when used for railroad ties, they burned quickly at very high temperatures and needed to be carefully monitored when used indoors.

The use of natural gas and automatic oil-fired stoves in our greater community increased in the 1950s and began to be found in my family's, extended family, and friends' homes. Prior to the advanced home heating systems, rising in the mornings shook one out of their somnolence during winter months. The earliest riser in the household had the task to start a fire in the heater to ameliorate the cold morning's temperature before other members arose.

Most homes in the neighborhood had minimal indoor sanitation conveniences. Though they had indoor toilets and a sink for hand and face washing, it was rare to have a bathtub or shower facility in many the *Bush* homes. If the latter were available, most flats lacked hot water to enjoy these amenities. Many families had to trek once a week to the local public park shower rooms to enjoy a warm shower. Or mothers hung bedsheets in the kitchen area to provide a semblance of privacy where each family member bathed in large metal tub filled with water that had been heated in a metal container on the kitchen stove then poured into the tub located on the floor.

If family wished to enjoy continuous and modern in-home hot water service, a water tank and water pipes had to be installed at the property owner's or renter's expense. An alternative was to heat water in a large metal container on the kitchen stove or heater and use as needed for bathing, washing clothes, or washing dishes. After my mother's pleading, I remember my father hired a plumber to help him install our first Rudd hot water heater tank in a corner of the kitchen, while we lived at 8932 S. Green Bay Avenue. It was like adding a family member to our household. Our expense was minimized because the water piping had been installed in the bungalow at least twenty years before but was never completed by the previous owner or renter.

Home laundry was a fastidious chore for women or anyone who had to do this task. Up until the 1950s, most households used a wood framed zinc or glass surface washboard to scrub laundry. Others incurred the expense and paid for home delivery laundry services. Only a few families owned an automatic electric washing machine. In time, more families were able to purchase one from our community stores. Our machine arrived while we were living in the *Bush* (1945-1950). It was placed in the back part of our flat sans a direct hot water system.

Similarly, dishwasher and dish dryer machines were practically unknown in neighborhood homes for decades. Households who had seven or more children would probably never have bought one due to the cost, and because washing and drying dishes was an expected chore for most family members. These chores were supposed to build character and teach responsibility for whoever's turn it was that week.

During my early youth, I rarely saw or entered a home that had an electric window unit or whole house air conditioning system though both were on the market since 1930s. Many households just pushed aside the curtains and raised the windows higher to allow more outside breezes to enter the room. Some families used small oscillating window or floor fans during Chicago's sweltering summer months.

Without the above cooling systems, workers lost precious sleep due to the night's oppressive heat. Yet rose in the morning to start the trek to their jobs. In the steel mills, the men faced more stifling heat as they worked long hours in the hot oven-like massive buildings made of corrugated sheet metal. Air conditioning at work was unheard of though huge fans were used, but these were mostly ineffective on the workers.

To counteract the heat in the mills, companies offered workers cellophane wrapped soft orange flavored sweet and salty candy. It was supposed to replenish the loss of sodium in their bodies while they were exposed to the stifling heat in the workplace. Many fathers brought these tangy candies home and the children swapped these delights between each other.

Steel workers had to get to work and insert their time cards into a timeclock to confirm their daily attendance and hours worked. They used different modes of travel to get to the mills and workers were ubiquitous in the neighborhood. They commuted by foot, personal vehicle, bicycle, public street car or bus. The latter two modes were only available on certain days and hours throughout the week, which was a challenge to workers whose schedule unexpectedly varied.

A regular work schedule meant one of a three-shift schedules in an eight hour day, i.e., 7 a.m. to 3 p.m., 3 p.m. to 11 p.m., 11 p.m. to 7 a.m., for low wages, seven days a week. Oftentimes they worked overtime on holidays with or without overtime pay variance. It was the Labor Unions that brought about justice for the workers as years passed and has endured in this industry even today.

During my early life, I never knew any congregant or friend who was employed in downtown Chicago where better paying jobs and better conditions could be found. Parents encouraged their sons and daughters to work in various steel mills and many found employment here. Others worked in local book and magazine printing companies, a cardboard box and paper cup factory, several small coal yards, scrap metal salvaging businesses, department stores, and small businesses offering every product or service and job vacancies were perennial.

Several "social functioning" organizations[82] such as fraternal clubs, churches, societies, or social events as discussed in Gillette's study, "common culture" existed everywhere. The groups were identical to those described by Innis-Jiménez' research. They evolved within the Mexican community in South Chicago into influential groups.

In the spiritual realm, as the Mexican families continued to remain in the area, they yearned to worship God in Spanish as they did in México by attending a *"Misa (Mass)"* in Spanish and Latin. For the Protestant Mexican, they yearned to attend a Spanish-speaking *"culto"* or *servicio"* (religious service) to fill their spiritual needs.

Some immigrants and emigrants knew about the Baptist ministry before arriving in Chicago. It had been introduced in Texas and México in earlier times. Deborah J. Baldwin indicates that[83] in 1839, American Protestant Evangelicals seriously considered outreach in México. The missionaries strategized how to launch their work in Texas first then created a "highway to México and South American populations" as their work moved through the Southwest and into Latino América. Their effort followed the expanding job opportunities in agriculture, railroad, steel production, granaries, and hotel work where Mexicans were found living and working.

Baldwin indicates work by the Southern Baptist Convention in the U.S. focused their interest on México as early as 1836. One of the earliest missionaries to México from Texas was a missionary Melinda Rankin, who originally hailed from the New England area. A review of her life's work is remarkably interesting and powerful, Christ-filled, and inspiring for what she accomplished in her era.

In time, other Protestant Christian denominations, conventions and respective leaders brought their missionary work to the Spanish-speaking people through this "great revival in the West." The revival by these groups and their work brought a simpler understanding to the immigrants of the meaning of being Christian in the footsteps of the Christ in an Evangelical Baptist setting.

Hispanic Leadership Recognition

As indicated earlier in this document, I have provided the names of Spanish-speaking pastors who ministered at *Iglesia Bautista Del Salvador* between 1926-1991, that is, from the very founding of this congregation until the year when it closed its doors. Though material is minimal, I was able to glean some information[84] about these pastors, their work and occasionally rare photographs and documents in which their names and images appear. I summarize some information in which they participated.

As stated above, the earliest pastors in *Iglesia Bautista Del Salvador* were: Rev. Felix T. Galindo, Rev. Carlos M. Gurrola, Rev. Florencio M. Santiago, and Rev. Miqueas D. Godínez. Information is referenced in, *American Baptists With a Spanish Accent*, written by Rev. Dr. Adam Morales in 1964. This publication is a rare historic research of the Spanish-speaking Baptist ministry in the U.S. from its beginnings until the year the research was published. I acquired a photocopy of this out-of-print work from Daniel Magaña, Dr. Morales' nephew in 2020. Daniel was a Christian friend of mine in Chicago for decades. We maintained communication and attended Spanish-speaking Baptist conventions and associations over several years. He was living in Virginia until mid-October 2021 when he left us at eighty-six years of age.

The above pastors and ad hoc pastors[85] names also appear in several of this congregation's anniversary programs. These include the fortieth (1966), fifty-first (1977), fifty-third (1979), sixtieth (1986), sixty-first (1987), sixty-second (1988), and the sixty-fifth (1991). These leaders represent a small number of many men who served in this church's ministry as it expanded in South Chicago and elsewhere.

In the fifty-first anniversary program, Rev. Gurrola is recognized as the second pastor of *Iglesia Bautista Del Salvador* without specific dates of service. In 1927, when just under thirty-years[86] of age, he was elected to be the first Spanish-speaking ordained Baptist minister assigned to work in the Chicago area. This is a year after the Mexican Baptist Church established its mission in South Chicago. Rev. Gurrola is also recognized as being the evangelist director of a radio broadcast program in Los Angeles, "*La Voz De Esperanza* (The Voice of Hope)," in the late 1920s, after having moved to this area.

A recent website posting in, *Convención de Iglesias Bautistas Hispanas* (Convention of Hispanic Baptist Churches), provides us some information about Rev. Gurrola. During his lifetime, he dedicated his work to Christian instruction and preparing men and women for Baptist ministry and teaching. He studied and graduated from various universities and seminary programs in México and California.

The website announcement informs us that he died in June 1988, in Alhambra, California, at ninety-years of age. During his lifetime, he and his wife, Guadalupe Garay Gurrola, a Baylor Baptist College alumna, established Gurrola Baptist Foundation, "*Fundación Bautista Gurrola*," a non-profit organization, in Pasadena California. It awards funds to Baptist men and women in the ministry or who retired from this field. It also supports seminarians, and laypersons who wish to prepare for Baptist Spanish-speaking ministry careers.

As stated above, Rev. Godínez is referenced as the sixth pastor, sans dates of service in *Iglesia Bautista Del Salvador* in various anniversary programs up to its sixty-fifth year (1991). Beyond his name being listed, we can only glean portions of his ministerial work, education preparation, or other congregations in which he may have served. His photo is rare and was not identified in the material I found about him. He may be present in photographs but is unmarked.

I remember the respect people had for Rev. Dr. Adam Morales when he visited the South Chicago congregation. He always brought inspiring, informative, and uplifting reports about his ministry as director of Spanish-speaking Work of American Baptist Home Mission Societies. He is recognized in some photos I present.

His responsibilities included work with Baptist Spanish-speaking conventions, associations, and congregations. He dedicated thirty-three years of active Baptist ministry. In March 1981, the *Convención's* Newsletter, *El Maná*[87] (The Manna) announced Dr. Morales passed away in California in late November in 1980. He was probably an octogenarian.

Dr. Adam's brother, Rev. Benjamín Morales and his wife, Rev. Ruth Morales, were ordained preachers and leaders in the Baptist ministry for decade in Los Angeles and elsewhere. Sometime in the late 1990s, my wife and I were fortunate to visit and hear Rev. Ruth Morales preach at a morning worship service in the Los Angeles Baptist Church where she pastored. We heard an inspiring message from this well-prepared Mexican American woman who was highly respected during her years of Baptist ministry.

Rev. Benjamín Morales engaged in Baptist higher education as an alum in the *Seminario Bautista Hispano-Americano* in Los Angeles. It focused on preparing Hispanic leaders within the denomination. He was elected president of this institution from 1954 to 1963. It closed in 1964, due to several issues that could not be resolved at the time: recruitment and training, budget constraints, employment of the seminarians after training, and the level of academics received by the students. Nonetheless, this organization continued with its critical program through a new and improved institution.

In 1990, my wife and I attended a service at Los Angeles Baptist church along with Rev. César O. Mascareñas, a pastor who brought many messages to *Iglesia Bautista Del Salvador* during the 1950s-1960s as a guest speaker. Upon retirement, after his wife died, he became a resident in Atherton Baptist Homes, in Alhambra, California. We visited him in 2017 as he continued to share the Word on a regular schedule with the retirees. He died in 2019 after decades of Baptist ministry. Though a small man in physical stature, he brought powerful messages to thousands of people to Christ.

Each of these men and women of Hispanic background are examples of servants who encouraged many youth to serve Christ. The Baptist effort in the South Chicago ministry was richly enhanced by their information, wisdom and spirit of Christ each consistently brought to this area of Spanish-speaking people.

In September 2020, Dinah Pérez, a granddaughter of one of our pastors, Rev. Pilar Muñoz, discovered a yellowed mostly intact and legible diploma awarded him in May 1935 from the *Seminario Bautista Hispano-Americano* in Los Angeles. He was twenty-nine-years of age when he graduated from this Christian institution. He went on to use this preparation to serve as pastor in various capacities in *Iglesia Bautista Del Salvador* in South Chicago including other ministries in and around the Chicago area for decades. More about his life is discussed later in this document.

Women in *Iglesia Bautista Del Salvador*, and their husbands, were noted and recognized for their leadership roles in many activities. It would take several pages to name and share the history of each of them. I recall here a few that impacted the lives of many parishioners in this congregation.

Some of their names are listed in various anniversary programs. I and others served with and personally knew these Christian sisters who modeled Christ in their lives and activities. Through them, many of us personally witnessed and understood the meaning of being a Christian role model and teacher-servant-leader.

One of these caring and tireless sisters in Christ was María de la Concepción Ambrosia Zavala de Martínez, better known as Mary Martínez (1914-2014), and affectionately known as *Concha*. Her husband was Ramón Martínez, a quiet man who shared his love for Christ and hard-earned living and wisdom in various programs and activities in this congregation for decades. He left us in 1979, just before his eightieth birthday. He was one of two Masons in our congregation which some of our church members seemed to frown upon though this did not affect their love and work for Christ.

Mary is seen in several historic pictures at Baptist Conventions and other conferences dating from the mid-1920s. I am grateful to her for providing me photographs of events which she attended in various states. She was active in South Chicago in many women's programs, singing in adult choir, and writing inspiring poems throughout her life. She is seen in several *Convención* photos I have included in this book.

During several Christmas seasons in the 1960s, Mary and Ramón donated evergreen trees to decorate the sanctuary. These filled the room with pine scent and were decorated with holiday lights. Beautiful potted poinsettias complemented the sanctuary as well. Our *Navidad* services were merry as the lyrics in a popular Christmas song teaches us.

Theresa Martínez, daughter of Mary and Ramón graciously provided me early photographs of youth who were members of this congregation. She also sent me two undated pieces of her mother's writings. One is titled, *"What Easter Means to Me."* Another piece I received shared Mary's talent in her bilingual wordsmithing of, *"Twas the Night Before Christmas (Mexican American Version)."* Also, I received two other pieces written by Mary, *"To My Family,"* and *"I Am Fine,"* written in 2004, a few years before her passing. Mary provided me verbal anecdotes and printed historical information about the men and women who participated in the early Baptist Christian evangelism effort in *Iglesia Bautista Del Salvador.*

She and the late Amelia Balderas (1926-2021), wife of Rev. Efraín Balderas, each worked over fifty years each in Spanish-speaking Baptist congregations. Amelia was active with her husband as he pastored here and elsewhere in various capacities. She volunteered in congregations in the area and other states until her passing in March 2021, while she was living with Terri Balderas Thomas, one of her daughters in New Jersey. Amelia was especially recognized for her work with women's groups as an officer and participant in several annual meetings of Hispanic American Baptist Conventions and Associations throughout the Midwest.

Amelia was an historian. She wrote comprehensive reports and maintained historical records of the Mexican Baptist work in Chicago and elsewhere. She, Mary Martínez, Elisa Dávila Pérez, wife of Frank Pérez, and several other Christian women could be seen regularly preparing programs to assure these events were well organized, and meaningful to and for the participants.

Another sister of the *Iglesia Bautista Del Salvador* who worked tirelessly for Christ here and elsewhere for years was Anita Sasso Fierro, a fine servant-leader. She received Christian education training for domestic and foreign missionary work at the Baptist Missionary Training School, located on the west side of Chicago.

Upon graduating, she arrived in South Chicago and soon met Jonathan Fierro whom she later married. He was the son of Jesús and Dolores Fierro, pioneer members of *Iglesia Bautista Del Salvador*. Jonathan was a constant associate who supported Anita's work in this congregation. Anita was a fine lady who was gifted with a beautiful coloratura soprano voice and a love for Christ. She used her voice to sing in our choral programs or as a soloist for many years. Her singing and piano ability always enhanced our music programs.

Her leadership with our children's programs was outstanding. She could be seen in the weekly Sunday morning program in the basement with this group while their parents received the Word in the sanctuary upstairs. In spite of having a daughter born with special needs, she and Jonathan raised her and three other beautiful children. Anita and her team leaders prepared programs with energy and Christ-centered themes which the children enjoyed over many years. She finished her earthly work in 1998, at sixty-eight years of age.

Our congregation was blessed to have another young Christian sister who grew up in South Chicago's working-class environment and lived in the *Bush* neighborhood most of her life. We all knew her as, "Susie," but her birth name was María de Jesús Apolinar. She and Anita Sasso Fierro were alumna from Baptist Missionary Training School in Chicago. Both of them focused on Christian missionary work.

Facilitator in Establishing the First Mexican Baptist Church in South Chicago

Susie was a bright and tall young Christian youth. She was raised in a typical Mexican American family culture as were most of us who attended the *Iglesia Bautista Del Salvador*. She was a vibrant young person who went on to marry a fine man who was a pastor, Rev. William Wells. Their evangelical ministry included working with Native Americans and other groups in various states. In 1997, she completed her earthly work in her late sixties after decades of serving Christ.

Another Christian woman leader in our congregation was Lydia Montemayor Rucoba. Her husband, Rodolfo "Rudy," was a devoted husband and spiritual servant-leader. Their work encompassed the children's ministry just around the time Anita Fierro arrived here. In time, Lydia and Rudy moved to Garland, Texas and began an extensive children's program in Dallas.

While living in Texas, they established a non-for-profit, Heights Lighthouse Apartment Ministry. Their summer Newsletter from 2002, *The Beacon*, describes their program to help underprivileged youth and their families to know about and live Christ. I am sure their program was modeled after experiences and mentoring they received in South Chicago Neighborhood House's programs in the *Bush* in their earlier years.

Lydia's Christian ministry on earth was completed in 1983 at eighty-three years of age. Rudy left us in 2013 at eighty-eight years of age. Lydia's parents were Rev. Tomás Montemayor (1905–1976) and Esther Montemayor.

Another tireless leader for Christ here for many years was "*la hermana* (sister)," Isabel Muñoz, wife of Rev. Muñoz. This stalwart sister came to this congregation from Kansas. She was a tall, elegant person who displayed strength and courage in women's activities from organizing and delivering exciting programs which inspired everyone to carry forth Christ's message.

In addition to the above women, I would like to share the names of some pastors I knew when they served in this congregation. One was Rev. Tomás Montemayor who served for many years. He and Pastor Muñoz co-shared the pulpit ministry about the time I began attending services here during the early 1950s. Pastor Montemayor was active in the various ministries before he left. He brought Christian-themed messages wherever he spoke which were full of wisdom and applicability to our daily and Christian living. Like other pastors here, he and his wife Esther raised a large, beautiful family in the area.

Pastor Muñoz was a minister here for years in addition to having other responsibilities in Christ-centered activities over decades in South Chicago and other cities. Pastor Muñoz baptized me in this church in the mid-1950s. He founded a new Spanish-speaking mission in the cavernous Hyde Park Baptist Church building. Puerto Rican families were settling in the area and were seeking a pastor and a worship center. He found this place that was once a middle-class English-speaking congregation. It was diminishing in membership and activities while the Spanish-speaking newcomers were increasing quickly.

I helped him in the music ministry in Hyde Park. The building where he established this work was located near the east terminus of the old elevated "L" train structure before it was modified along 63rd Street and Stony Island Avenue. I played the majestic pipe organ in the large sanctuary for several Sunday afternoons and at other services.

He also led a nascent Spanish-speaking Baptist Ministry in Mount Prospect, Illinois, during the late 1950s. I often rode with him and others to and from this ministry. Rev. Muñoz had a deep commitment and an incessant love for humanity to know and live for Christ.

He and his wife had five children: two girls and three boys. The eldest daughter, Rhoda, completed a Master's Degree in Education from Governors State University, in Illinois, as did her husband, Antonio Pérez. Along the way, they decided to move to Puerto Rico with one of their sons Juan (John). Dinah and Antonio Marcus remained in Chicago with their grandparents, to continue their university studies.

In Puerto Rico, Rhoda soon learned and led an American Sign Language Program in Spanish to teach local children and adults who needed this important communication skill in Hatillo, a municipality in Puerto Rico. Her effective program operated for many years until her passing in mid-May 2020, just before her eighty-second birthday. Other leaders in Puerto Rico continued Rhoda's valuable work.

Pastor Muñoz' son-in-law Antonio, and his sons and daughter were actively involved in numerous programs in *Iglesia Bautista Del Salvador* for many years. We previously alluded to Dinah Pérez and her piano assistance in our services. Years later, after Pastor Muñoz' wife, Isabel, passed away in Chicago, he moved to Hatillo. In 1994, he passed on to his heavenly home in his mid-eighties and is buried here. In late spring, 2022, Antonio, an octogenarian, moved to Mississippi to live with his son, John and his family.

Hispanic Baptist Conventions and Associations

The history of this congregation was founded by the few Mexicans who settled in South Chicago a few years after this ethnic group arrived in this neighborhood[88]. Some of the surviving records speak of their efforts to begin serving and meeting their social and spiritual needs. It was important for them to support their brothers and sisters in Christ. They convened gatherings in South Chicago to encourage one another, share the Gospel and discuss ordinary life events.

This effort was supported by the American Baptist and Home Missions Work and Baptist associations. These organizations focused on the growth of nascent groups and wished to help in as many areas of need that could be mutually achieved.

Mexican immigrants and emigrants continued to come to South Chicago for many decades. They arrived not only from México, but from Texas, Kansas, Indiana, Michigan, Missouri, and Nebraska. I found this peculiarity in many of the congregants of *Iglesia Bautista Del Salvador* whom I personally knew as I worshipped here.

Over the years, their leaders encouraged them to participate in Spanish-speaking *convenciones* and *asociaciones* and about spreading the Gospel as English-speaking Baptists churches were successfully doing for decades. Their work is discussed in this book.

Documents I found of their events speak of topics on which the Mexicans focused. These included Christian living, salvation of their souls, the Sacrament of baptism by emersion and celebrating Holy Communion, the importance of linking their work with contemporary and future believers, hymnody, tithing, development of effective laypersons into leaders within their congregations, studying and understanding the Books of the Old and New Testament, serving Christ through active involvement and supporting worldwide Baptist activities.

Their meetings brought together conventioneers from a variety of backgrounds. Seminars were led by local and international pastors. Participants were men and woman laypeople, and youth of all ages. These events met at least once a year in various cities and states. They delved into lively discussions about how to implement the above themes and how to facilitate and strengthen their work to reach others through evangelistic efforts. They emphasized *eslabonaje* (linkage), and *servicio* (service) in and for Christ with Baptist and other believers.

One of the earliest sources of information about such events is discussed in a document titled, *Breve Historia De La Convención Bautista Hispano-Americana Y Constitución De La Misma* (Brief History of the Hispanic American Baptist Convention and Its Constitution). It was published in June 1965 by Rev. Efraín L. Balderas, Historian, in South Chicago, Illinois, during their thirty-seventh *Convención Anual*. Mary Martínez shared it with me in 2014. I thought someday I might use this document if I ever wrote about the Mexican Baptists.

It is written in English and Spanish. It shows an original Budget of $107, in July 1928. It was published on the fortieth anniversary of the *Convención's* founding. Its brief history states that the *Convención* was actually organized in *the Primera Iglesia Bautista Mexicana El Salvador* in South Chicago on January 7, 1928. This is two years after this congregation transitioned from being a mission to the fully registered congregation as we have stated earlier. It contains two rare black and white photographs of the original Board of Directors, under its original name, *Convención Bautista Mexicana Del Norte De Norte América* (Mexican Baptist Convention of the North of North America).

This was an interesting name which seems to indicate that the organizers were thinking effectively of reaching beyond the few states in which they were spreading the gospel. In the future, this name was changed to, *Convención Bautista Hispano-Americana*, probably being more inclusive for reaching all Spanish-speaking Christians as opposed to only focusing on the Mexican cohort.

A second photograph in the above *Constitución* was taken in 1928-1929. It shows its new board of directors: President, Rev. Florencio M. Santiago; Vice President, Rev. F. T. Galindo; Secretary, L. H. Briones; Treasurer: Ms. Sarita Buzo, and Historian: J. A. González. I may have personally met Rev. Santiago, but none of the others. All of these persons surely visited the Mexican Baptist congregation in South Chicago whenever these conventions were celebrated here over the years. I have no doubt that these leaders attended other Christian gatherings in Illinois, Indiana, Michigan, and Latin American countries.

In June 1974, the *Convención* met to celebrate their forty-sixth *Convención Anual* in Scottsbluff, Nebraska. The conventioneers travelled via their personal vehicles as I remember the South Chicago delegates did. When we attended these meetings, it was on our own travel expense. We were hosted in the homes of local congregants and enjoyed home meals to offset our lodging and food costs. No specific congregation name is seen in the picture but it was probably hosted in the Scottsbluff Mexican Baptist church as was customary during conventions.

In the 1974 edition of *El Maná*, the official publication of the *Convención*, we find two resolute pastors who led in preparing this document and who served in South Chicago, cities in Illinois, Indiana, and other states. The publisher was Rev. Efraín L. Balderas, and Rev. Miguel A. Castillo, director whose pictures I have included in this work. There were six states that composed the *Convención*: Illinois, Indiana,

Kansas, Michigan, Nebraska, and Wisconsin. *El Maná* emphasized the importance of the *Convención* and belief that God would provide immensely to those who attended these annual team building and leadership events.

Rev. Jacobo A. Thome was the president of the *Convención* in 1971. He preached at many services in South Chicago. It convened in Chicago in June 1978, to celebrate their fiftieth anniversary, at the *Primera Iglesia Bautista Latino Americana*. Rev. Thome was the pastor of this host congregation. A few members from *Iglesia Bautista Del Salvador* attended this service.

The anniversary program names the fifty-one presidents[89] of the *Convención* over the fifty years of existence (1928–1978), with some serving double terms. The asterisk (*) indicates that this brother also served as the pastor of the *Iglesia Bautista Del Salvador,* but not necessarily in the actual year of service.

Presidents of The Convención Bautista Hispana-Americana 1928-1978

1928 Carlos M. Gurrola*
1929 Florencio M. Santiago
1930 Agusín Apra
1931 José P. Ruíz
1932 Carlos M. Gurrola
1933 José P. Ruíz
1934 Armando M. Alvarado*
1935 Ramón Tolosa
1936 Armando V. Alvarado
1937 Adam Morales
1938 Porfírio Martínez
1939 Porfírio Martínez
1940 Pilar Muñoz*
1941 Samuel B. Colón
1942 Florencio M. Santiago
1943 Tomás Montemayor*
1944 Florencio M. Santiago

1945 Cástulo De Lara
1946 Cástulo de Lara
1947 Armando V. Alvarado
1948 Florencio M. Santiago
1949 Vahac Mardirosián
1950 Ramón Tolosa
1951 Ramón Trejo
1952 Samuel Hernández B.
1953 Cesar O. Mascareñas
1954 Florencio M. Santiago
1955 Jim Macías
1956 Eleucadio Méndez
1957 Francisco Lémus
1958 Miguel A. Castillo
1959 Isaías Hernández Loera
1960 Miguel A. Castillo
1961 Efraín L. Balderas

1962 Efraín Balderas
1963 Félix T. Galindo
1964 Miguel A. Castillo
1965 Alfonso Ramírez
1966 Alfonso Ramírez
1967 Humberto Salinas*
1968 Humberto Salinas
1969 Pedro Álvarez
1970 Florencio M. Santiago
1971 Jacobo A. Tohme
1972 Ángel Ojeda
1973 A.V. Ramírez
1974 Isaías Hernández
1975 Isaías Hernández
1976 Isaías Hernández
1977 Armando L. González
1978 A. V. Ramírez

Facilitator in Establishing the First Mexican Baptist Church in South Chicago

Another organization provided leadership to South Chicago Baptist Spanish and other churches in the area. It was the "*Asociación Bautista Lagunera* (Lake Area Baptist Association)." I could not find information on its history as to when it was established, by whom, its goals, mission, and when it stopped operating. After some time, I learned that this *Asociación* served to complement the ministries of the *Convención,* as discussed earlier, but more at the local level.

Many of the pastors and other men and women leaders who were involved in the *Convención* activities were actively involved in the *Asociación*. At times, these leaders served simultaneously as current or past officers within these two and other groups. They were tireless in fulfilling their leadership responsibilities during their quarterly meetings. Each gathering was theme-based on Biblical references. I attended several of these events at which I and others played the piano during the singing sessions.

I found four programs about their events. The earliest program relates to their meeting held on Saturday, 8:00 a.m.-6:30 p.m., August 24, 1957, in *Primera Iglesia Bautista Mexicana*, East Chicago, Indiana. The full-day's theme was, "*Llenando Nuestras Obligaciones Como Testigos de Cristo* (Meeting our Obligations as Christ's Witnesses)." It is based on the fifth book in the Bible's New Testament, the Acts of the Apostles, 1: 8, which reads: "But you shall receive power when the Holy Spirit comes upon you, and you shall be my witnesses both in Jerusalem and in all Judea and Samaria, and unto the uttermost part of the earth."

The program does not indicate the name of the pastor of the host congregation, but the names of five pastors from other *Asociación* congregations are listed, including the name of the special speaker from a mission sponsored by the *Asociación* in México. Each pastor was scheduled to lead discussions and devotionals throughout the day's meetings related to the above theme.

After each speaker presented his message on a portion of the pre-assigned theme, a brief open discussion was held. I remember this part of these activities as it allowed the conferees an opportunity to share their thoughts on what the speaker expressed in his message. It was interesting to listen and learn from these discussions. Two pastors who worked in South Chicago, Rev. Efraín L. Balderas, and Rev. Ralph Bratton, delivered their thoughts on the theme. I do not remember if anyone took pictures of the speakers as they spoke. We will read about the participation of these pastors in other such events.

The second *Asociación Bautista Lagunera* program describes one that occurred on Saturday morning, March 1, 1958, on our campus, *Iglesia Bautista Del Salvador,* in South Chicago. My pencil notes on the program indicate that one-hundred-sixty-seven people attended this event, with fifty-five from our congregation.

The theme of the meeting was, "*Llenando Nuestros Deberes en el Campo Misionero* (Meeting Our Duties in the Missionary Field)," with no Biblical reference noted. This was a perfect theme as our congregation had always supported Baptist Foreign Mission work in México, and other Latin American nations in liaison with laypersons, ordained personnel, and in-country faith-based organizations.

Several *Asociación* congregations were represented at the event composed of adults, and youth. Pastors who had led our congregation in earlier years participated in this event as Rev. Efraín L. Balderas, and Rev. Ralph Bratton, and other visiting pastors. Also, there was a host of visiting speakers. My future father-in-law, Juan Bautista Rivera, a recent resident to South Chicago from Puerto Rico was one of the lay speakers. He was a life-long Christian who worked tirelessly for the Faith and people in many other such programs. Other laypersons were assigned to make presentations during the eleven-o-clock period. Simultaneous quarterly meetings of women, men, and youth from this congregation and visiting groups were also held throughout the day.

The third program I have in my files about the *Asociación Bautista Lagunera* describes a meeting held the morning of May 20, 1958, in the First Baptist Church, Waukegan, Illinois. The sessions on specific topics were conducted from early morning hours until early evening. Rev. Miguel Castillo was the life-long pastor in the Spanish-speaking congregation in this lakeside city north of Chicago. He left this Earth in February 1992 at seventy-three years of age.

The theme for the meeting was, "*Nuestra Obra Misionera Ante La Inquietud Mundial* (Our Mission During the World's Uneasiness)," with the Biblical reference from an Old Testament Bible reference, II Kings, 6:16: "Don't be afraid," the prophet Elisha answered, "Those who are with us are more than those who are with them."

Perhaps this theme attempted to reflect the many local and world-wide events that were taking place in 1958: NASA established, NASA launches Explorer I, Mr. Nikita Khrushchev became the head of the USSR, Soviet Union launched Sputnik 3, the microchip invented, USS Nautilus crossed under the North Pole, unemployment was over 7.0%, the Cha, Cha, Cha dance became a world craze, and Elvis Presley had already become a local and international sensation. The world was in flux and many pastors must have referenced these events in their homilies.

I remember adults and youth from our congregation attended the meeting as representatives to the *Asociación Bautista Lagunera*. To get to First Baptist Church of Waukegan, some conferees travelled north in cars along the shoreline of Lake Michigan. Another group of us met early Saturday morning at the Illinois Central Electric Train station platform at E. 91st and Baltimore Avenue in South Chicago.

We travelled to Van Buren station in downtown Chicago and deboarded the train. From here, we walked to Union Station and boarded the North Shore Electric Line to Waukegan. This whole trip must have taken almost two hours to reach our destination.

The goal of the event was to support the Hispanic Baptist ministry in this church. The sessions were held bilingually in Spanish and English. We heard some new and former speakers who once worked as full-time or ad hoc pastors in South Chicago: pastors Rev. Rafael Bratton, and Rev. Dr. Adam Morales and many other speakers.

A Fourth *Asociación Bautista Lagunera* program was celebrated at 9:00 a.m., Saturday, February 28, 1959. It was hosted in the *Primera Iglesia Bautista Latino-Americana*, located on the Westside of

Chicago, an area with a high population then and now, of long-time and recently arrived Latino immigrants. The pastor was, Rev. Dr. Dino Badaracco, an up-and-coming pastor to the Baptist Spanish-speaking community. He came to Chicago from a South American republic a few years before coming to this church and before we first met him.

The general theme of this quarterly meeting was, "*Buscando A Jehová* (Seeking Jehovah)," based on the Old Testament Psalm 17:8, "Keep me as the apple of the eye, hide me under the shadow of thy wings." Various pastors expounded their thoughts on this incisive theme as, seeking Jehovah (God) at home, work, one's congregation and community. Three pastors were key speakers: Rev. Efraín L. Balderas, Rev. Rafael Bratton, and Rev. Pedro Cruz, a recent pastor chosen to lead our *Iglesia Bautista Del Salvador* congregation in South Chicago. Other men and women laypersons, pastors, and youth leaders also led assigned activities throughout the event.

A more comprehensive history of *Asociación Bautista Lagunera* is unavailable. I believe it is important to understand its role in the development of the Spanish-speaking Baptist during the decades during which it was active. It would provide information as to what this organization accomplished in teaching about the Christ to the Spanish-speaking population and leadership development by their pastors and other leaders.

By knowing their history, we can understand the important liaison between the *Convención Bautista Hispana-Americana* and the many congregations and associations which partnered with them in their activities. It made their missions effective and stronger in a Christian symbiotic relationship by uniting and strengthening Baptist Spanish-speaking congregations in cities throughout Illinois, Michigan, and Indiana.

Many of the pastors named above knew that one day they would retire from the Baptist ministry. They understood it was important to seek young men who might consider entering full-or-part-time service. I recall this concern was an on-going theme in many of our youth events, annual conventions, associations or when the opportunity presented itself during one-on-one discussions.

Rev. Castillo was an advocate for recruiting young men to enter the Baptist ministry. He consistently presented this theme as he visited the various activities and congregations. He emphasized the need was great in those years and would continue in the future as the Spanish-speaking populations were projected to increase. His vision on the need for pastors was correct.

I believe Moisés López was the only male from our congregation who was ordained here and dedicated himself as a part-or full-time pastor. A few of us men served in supportive positions within this congregation as deacons or teachers. I was fortunate to preach twice during the 1960s when a pastor was unavailable. People said I did well.

I served here for many years. I was in the music ministry as pianist, organist, choir director, Sunday school teacher, camp counselor, and deacon. In later years, I was appointed Christian education director and deacon in an English-speaking Baptist congregation in Alexandria, Virginia when we lived there. It would be valuable to see current data on whether Baptist seminaries and Bible institutes have increased their training of more Hispanic men and women and into ministerial and other fields.

Pastor Castillo had several key assignments with many Baptist organizations. Among them were the American Baptist Association, *Convención Bautista Hispana-Americana*, and the *Asociación Bautista Lagunera* in the Chicago area. These allowed him carte blanche to advance and complete his work. I often wondered why young women were not encouraged to enter the pastoral ministry at the same level as men. In time, I learned this ministry was historically a male-centered tradition for centuries and is static today in many Protestant churches and in the Roman Catholic faith.

Asociación Lagunera held an annual meeting in our church on Saturday morning, October 29, 1977. This fall event brought many conventioneers from Illinois and Indiana where they participated in seminars on the organization's milestone activities and suggested directions for moving the Christian message forward in future years . The day-long gathering used the entire campus, from the balcony to the basement. I present these photographs of two prominent pastors who led parts of this meeting along with many other ministers. For decades, each provided leadership at this and other *Asociación* and *Convención* annual meetings.

Rev. Efraín Balderas next to the Chickering piano in between seminar presentation at the 1977 *Asociación* meeting. He served as pastor in South Chicago in the 1950s. (Béloz, 1977.)

Rev. Miguel Castillo, pastor, mentor, and American Baptist representative to the Spanish-speaking churches. He was an officer for years in the *Convención* and *Asociación* meetings. (Béloz, 1977.)

These annual meetings were successful because of the effort the officers of the *Asociación* expended to plan and coordinate the many discussion and study sessions for the day-long event. They did it without having the technology available such as conference calling, ZOOM or any of the many modern communication applications commonly used today. Yet, they were effective overall.

The women of our church were also a critical element to the success of this and other such days. They brought together their best Mexican and American cuisine skills to the kitchen and served these at our long tables in the basement to the conventioneers up to three meals that day. They prepared the entire menu in our simple kitchen.

Their important contribution started with breakfast of *"pan dulce y café"* (similar to coffee and Danish), *"almuerzo"* (lunch), and a

Facilitator in Establishing the First Mexican Baptist Church in South Chicago

light *"cena"* (evening meal) as the conventioneers prepared to return home. The team this day included Lee Armas, Martha López Marcano, Isabel Muñoz, conventioneer woman and some youth volunteers. Women were our champions whenever *Asociación, Convención* or other large or small gatherings meetings were held in South Chicago. They made us proud of their contribution for decades.

Youth Activities

The youth of *Iglesia Bautista Del Salvador* were actively involved in this congregation's programs over many decades. A youth-focused ministry existed since this congregation's earliest years. I believe our young people took to heart what Apostle Paul said in his Epistle to the Colossians 4:12: "Let no man despise thy youth; be thou an example of the believers, in word, in conversation, in charity, in spirit, in faith, in purity."

This verse is referenced in the fifty-third anniversary celebration of the *Convención* 1926-1979. It was in 1926 when two young men, Francisco Villagrana, and José Soledad, took the interest to meet with the pastor of the First Baptist Church of South Chicago, Rev. Edgar Woolhouse. While we have no pictures of them and this is the only reference we have about these two youth, what a difference they made in the history of the birth of this Mexican Baptist congregation.

Being young people did not dissuade them to discuss the topic of establishing a Spanish-speaking Mission in this congregation. Youth activities[90] expanded over the years to reach other youth beyond South Chicago. The various programs I have reviewed indicate they were allotted time during the *convenciones* and *asociaciones* to develop activities to support their Baptist youth interests.

During mid-1950s-1960s, Chicagoland Youth for Christ activities grew. Hundreds of Spanish-speaking youth attended these once-a-month Friday evening events. At these activities, we heard exciting youth pastors sharing reasons and examples of why Christian living was important to one's life, the joy and value to our lives of living in

Christ's image, and the Biblical assurances and blessings of our personal salvation. We also learned about the importance of sharing with others what we had discovered in the preachers' and Christian teachers' messages. The essence was to spread the Gospel to all who would listen.

Around the period as above, the Spanish-speaking and bilingual youth leaders expressed the desire to have a similar region-wide program. They named it Latin Youth for Christ (*Joventud Latina Para Cristo*). This group focused on the same verse expressed in Apostle Paul's letter to the Corinthians about being young and using this strength to live and honor God and Christ.

This evangelistic effort brought together Spanish-speaking and bilingual youth from a variety of congregations in the Chicago area not only the Baptist fellowships. This included Mennonite, Methodist, Lutheran, and Presbyterian Latino believers. They were our spiritual brothers and sisters. Our monthly meetings were celebrated at their houses of worship who graciously opened their doors to us.

Shortly after Latin Youth for Christ was organized, I was surprised to be selected as the main pianist to accompany the singing at these meetings. We sang from the book, *Youth Sings*[91], *A Praise Book of Hymns and Choruses*. It was used for the first time at the Friday night program on April 6, 1956, at the Mennonite house of worship, where the young pastor Rev. Mario O. Snyder, a bilingual and bicultural Argentinian by birth, brought us an inspiring message. I noted this event on the cover of my song book that night. Our theme song was derived from the Chisholm and Lowden hymn, "Living for Jesus." It was often sung at all our hour-and-a-half spirit-filled meetings.

The message of this beautiful chorus encouraged youth to choose a pathway in our lives that honors Jesus in all we do and thereby be a blessing to Him for what He did on for us on the cross. These words and their meaning were important then and remain so seven decades later.

These gatherings were mostly attended by high school teenagers from the congregations cited above. It was our opportunity to come together to hear the Gospel by Christian leaders who inspired us to be Christlike while we were living in our salad days. We enjoyed hearing a gratuitous selection of songs by visiting groups and learned new ones to be sung at our home youth gatherings. We enjoyed group and personal prayer time and committed to be faithful messengers and doers of Christ's work throughout our lives.

Latin Youth for Christ meetings helped many youth to anchor their personal faith in Him as a believer. We were encouraged to grow in faith by reading, understanding and applying the truths of the Scriptures to our lives and to take Christ to others even if we were young people.

In addition to these monthly meetings, our congregation's youth group celebrated its own special events from time to time. Annually, during Christmas season we joined the choir members as they went caroling during a few cold nights to the homes of various congregation members. Sometimes we travelled to nearby neighborhoods in our cars to spread Christmastide carols. It was a delight when some of the residents of the homes where we stopped would come out to thank us by serving hot chocolate to warm us for the surprise appearance.

During the fall season we would travel to Dan Ryan Woods to enjoy a hay wagon ride and marshmallow roast with a cohort of teenagers and a several adults who enjoyed being out of doors for a couple of evening hours. Our church celebrated an annual July 4th event in a nearby public park in Hammond, Indiana. After a day full of sports activities and eating to the limits, the pastor would bring us together to hear a message with a Christian theme and send us on our return trip to South Chicago.

I remember one event when three youth invested their energy to prepare the basement of our building where one of our programs was scheduled to be held. These were Paul Gonsález, Daniel M. López, and I. This was in the mid-1950s while we were enrolled in Bowen High School. Little did we realize the effort and time it would take to prepare this venue in order to receive our guests.

We washed, mopped, rinsed, and waxed the plastic tile covered floor, and finally buffed it to perfection, using a powerful electric buffing machine on most of the three-thousand square feet basement floor. We were very careful that the spinning buffer did not injure us neophyte custodians. Luckily, we completed our project the night before the scheduled event. This respite gave us time to recover physically from our youthful stint. We were pleased our effort was recognized on the night of the meeting.

In future years after high school, each of us went on to begin our lives that would prepare us to become successful adults. Paul and I each married young women from our congregation. We both served in the U.S. Army. He was deployed to Viet Nam, and I to Germany.

Paul earned a Bachelor's and Master's Degrees from universities in Illinois and an international university. I earned a Bachelor's and Master's degree in Spanish Language and Literature from Illinois State University. I was awarded a full-time postgraduate fellowship which helped me earn a Ph.D. in Education at Southern Illinois University, Carbondale, Illinois.

After college, Daniel entered the business sector and became co-publisher and publisher of *NUESTRO Magazine* (Our Magazine), in New York City. His work was one of the early Latino magazines that was leading the way for Spanish-speaking people who chose to maintain their Hispanic roots but preferred to read printed material in English. The first issue of the magazine appeared in April 1977 and was published for several years.

Today, after many successful and exciting years of professional, including worldwide experience, we live in retirement in different States in our octogenarian years with the vicissitudes and blessings that accompany aging.

I find special joy when I reminisce about our youthful life in South Chicago. These include years of worshipping and serving Christ in *Iglesia Bautista Del Salvador*, and other congregations wherever I lived. Even more delightful is when I recall the names of Christian laypeople, pastors, youth, women, musicians and others with whom I had the personal opportunity and pleasure of knowing, growing and working with on- and off-campus. I hope my contribution to local Baptist history might confirm what we contributed and advanced was all for Christ and His kingdom.

In summary, as expressed by doctor and evangelist, Luke, in Chapter 10, Verse 27, we did so because we wished and strove to *"love the Lord our God with all our heart, soul, strength, and mind, and loved helping our neighbor as much as we loved ourselves."*

PART V: FOUNDING OF COMMUNITY CHRISTIAN CHURCH OF CHICAGO (1960)

This Part of the book[92] discusses the history and nascence of the above congregation. A major transformation occurred within *Iglesia Bautista Del Salvador* that is not referenced nor discussed in *Reseñas Históricas,* nor other written histories about this congregation.

I believe it is useful for us to briefly review a dynamic transition in a congregation to comprehend how God works when major decisions are made by Christians and the positive outcome of a particular one.

A significant event occurred on Wednesday evening during a congregational business meeting on June 8, 1960, thirty-four years after *Iglesia Bautista Del Salvador* was founded. My wife and I attended this meeting. As happens in some organizations, including religious groups, differences arise in personal or group understanding or perceptions of the essentials of their mission or goals which can modify the life of an entity.

Pastor Rev. Pedro Cruz presided over the meeting accompanied by deacons of the congregation. On the agenda that evening was a motion that apparently had been percolating in the congregation and needed to be discussed and resolved. Some expressed their sentiment that an issue was dividing the spirit and ultimately the work here. Some speakers stated that this congregation had neglected the essence, responsibilities and practices found in biblical theology as Christians.

All who wished to participate in the discussion were allowed to do so. Speakers were asked to stand and express their thoughts. After this was completed, a motion was called to order for the final vote. The motion was passed with a decision to separate from this Baptist congregation. Several members voted to leave and others decided to remain. Interestingly, my wife and I were married by Pastor Cruz in the sanctuary of this building just four months before this meeting. We voted to stay and continue to serve and worship God, Christ and the community. A prayer was raised and the meeting ended. I recall some members wept quietly as they departed. I remember seeing the sun fading through the slightly raised multi-colored lancet stained-glass windows on the west side of the sanctuary.

It was difficult to see some of our long-time friends and loved ones leave the meeting. Many of us were grieved but in spite of this pain, we were confident that our God would work in His mysterious way and this event would have a positive outcome. We had to trust and accept what transpired and moved forward with our Christian mission. It seemed that Pastor Cruz might be selected to lead the nascent group. However, his appointment was not secured and shortly thereafter moved elsewhere.

As the summer continued, some of the group who decided to leave agreed to meet in private home to celebrate Christian meetings. They met in the basement of the residence owned by Juan Bautista Rivera and Ignacia Rivera, who had recently become my in-laws. Their home was located just outside of South Chicago.

From the outset of their new life, this little group thanked God for all His blessings. They prayed He would help them find a pastor to lead them to worship Him as they believed in their understanding and interpretation of the Bible and felt in their minds and hearts. Their other priority was to locate a building in which to worship God and grow in their Christian evangelistic effort.

In time, they found a young pastor, Albert Young, and located their first building in the mid-1960s-1970s, in a nearby neighborhood. They named their congregation the Jeffery Manor Community Christian Church. When Pastor Young resigned, brother Ranulfo Garza became their leader for some years with the help of other members. Brother Young died some time in California in the late 1990s. Brother Garza suddenly died in mid-December 2020, from COVID-19, in Eagle Pass, Texas.

After some ten years at this location (1960-1970), the leadership decided to vacate Jeffery Manor. As the neighborhood demographics continued to change congregants were often faced with unfavorable personal incidents around their building. The decided to find a new site. They found a large vacant piece of property in Hegewisch neighborhood near the local electric train station. However, other factors and voices intervened which caused them to lose this opportunity. Nonetheless, their spirits were undiminished.

During part of the above decade, I was Division Director for the Ada S. McKinley Community Services, a non-for-profit organization when I learned of their experience and need. I spoke with the new Pastor, Steve Martínez (1949-) and informed him that the South Chicago Neighborhood House building was in my administrative area of responsibility and it might be available to them.

He and his team met with McKinley organization directors and subsequently signed a contract to rent parts of the above site. They used it for several years and celebrated their main services in the small campus gymnasium. They also used other rooms in this two-storied brick multi-building complex in the *Bush* neighborhood.

While the site was crowded it met most of their needs. While here, their attendance continued to grow. This created a need to locate a new site to continue and expand their current and future services.

In time, one of the congregation's leaders, Leopoldo Alvelo, learned about the availability of renting space in the former South Chicago Masonic Temple. It is a Hatzfeld designed four-story brick building in the Craftsman, prairie, revival style located at 2939 E. 91st Street.

This site was just one block south and two streets west of where *Iglesia Bautista Del Salvador* was located. It had not been a Masonic Temple since 1975 until the Mexican Community Committee became the new owner. It was a non-for-profit organization led by a long-time community leader, Henry Martínez.

After pastor Steve Martínez left the pulpit in late 1985, a new pastor was sought who would lead the congregation forward. In the interim, Sunday morning and evening messages were brought by a host of ad hoc visiting pastors and a few congregation lay persons.

During this period, one of these visiting speakers included a young man, who was in his thirties, brother Ricardo Ayala. Around fall of 1986 he was considered and was ultimately chosen as pastor. He hailed from El Salvador, San Salvador, Central America and was in the Chicago area.

The congregation officials directed a cohort from the congregation to meet with Henry Martínez to discuss the possibility of renting space in the above building. Ultimately, these were brother Ayala, Lydia Rivera, a community leader Elena Berezaluce Mulcahy, and others.

The Jeffery Manor congregation soon signed a contract for three years (1985-1988) with the Mexican Community Committee which benefited both organizations. Somewhere along the way, Jeffery Manor Christian Church changed its name to Community Christian Church of Chicago and continues use this name going forward. This action occurred either before or after this agreement was signed or after it moved from this site to an East Side campus.

The three-story brick Classical Revival building was dedicated by the Masons on Saturday, September 12, 1916, ten years before *Iglesia Bautista Del Salvador* was founded, and four days before the one-hundred-sixth anniversary of México's independence from Spain.

Though the building was a potential venue in the heart of South Chicago it has had many challenges. It had an elevator but it was not operating at the time the new renters moved in. All who came to the services Sunday morning and evening services had to ascend a long stairway in order to reach the third floor where their religious and other services were held. A large windowless inner room on this floor was used as their general worship area. Other smaller rooms on this floor were used for their Christian education activities. The venue was not for sale at that point in time. The leaders were undeterred by the challenges they endured while they met in this venue.

Brother Ayala was the Pastor here for some twenty-one years (1986-2007), along with his wife, Nancy Lee, and their three young children. He was ordained a Pastor in the Community Christian Church of Chicago ministry during his tenure. His bilingual skills in Spanish and

English served him to effectively spread the Gospel when he was coordinator of a Spanish-speaking radio ministry at Moody Bible Institute. He graduated from this Institute.

Under Pastor Ayala's leadership and direction from the elders and the congregant's approval, the wandering years without a permanent building came to fruition for this congregation as discussed earlier.

After he left the pulpit here, he continued to lead a couple of local Baptist congregations in the South East side of Chicago. He ultimately retired from the Baptist ministry in 2018 and continued to live in the community.

After Pastor Ayala left the pulpit, a lay leader Jimmy Serrano served in an interim appointment for some four years. Under his leadership, the congregation strove to advance Christ's work in its various ministries: preaching, teaching, music, youth, children, adults, and a variety outreach activities on-and-off campus in the surrounding neighborhood. The congregation continued to seek for a full-time pastor to further its Christian ministry to the community.

A Permanent Building Is Found (1988)

As Christians will attest, God incessantly provides. This happened on April 7, 1988[93], as Community Christian Church of Chicago purchased an almost seventy-five-year-old building located at 10323 S. Ewing Avenue, Chicago, Illinois. This milestone culminated the twenty-eight-year journey (1960-1988) of this congregation. Some said it compared minimally to the forty-years which the Israelites endured in the desert before reaching their Promised Land described in the Old Testament Books of Numbers and Deuteronomy. The Dedication of the building would take place some fourteen months in the future as discussed below.

The building was owned by the former East Side United Methodist Church/First Evangelical United Brethren Church which was founded by German and Swedish immigrants. They built their first building in 1876. In 1914, they moved into their second structure and remained here until around 1995 when they moved to their third new modern building and campus at 110th and S. Ewing Avenue. The old building was occupied by various secular groups for some thirty-four years before it was sold to the new owners.

Community Christian Church of Chicago paid ninety-thousand dollars in cash for the two-story brick structure and a small adjacent lot. It was purchased in this manner in order to avoid years of extra financing costs incurred in a regular mortgage. This transaction was possible because of God's unfailing support and continuous years of spiritual vision, tithing efforts of its members, former pastors, lay persons, officers, and contributions by friends. The building was a fixer-upper with great potential to serve God, and the spiritual needs of the congregation and residents in the surrounding neighborhoods.

Prior to 1988, I was unaware of the East Side United Methodist Church nor the history of the building and its future relationship with the Community Christian Church of Chicago, my in-laws, and me. I remember seeing this impressive building for years but thought nothing of it. Now, I yearned to learn about its history.

In 2015, while visiting the Southeast Chicago Historical Society's Museum I found and bought a copy of the book titled, *Chicago's Southeast Side Cultural Institutions: A Community of Churches*. It was published a few years earlier by the Museology Class of the local Washington High School. One of the pictures in it shows an early photograph of East Side United Methodist Church and many other church buildings including a brief story about each. I was elated that it contained a picture of this building to help me identify any exterior modifications.

Viewing the façade on South Ewing Avenue, one readily sees that some major structural changes have been made over the decades. It is a rectangular single-storied grey concrete block building and has a basement. It is designed in an Italianate façade and adorned with complimentary long rectangular columns and lintels topping these and were used on it elsewhere .

Noticeably missing from the façade is a large original double-arched stained-glass window. It was located in the center of the west wall. It was removed and sealed over with grey concrete cement blocks that match the original materials of the building. We have no history as to when this happened.

A modification was made to the lower section of this window. The slanted cornice (ledge) just above it has been removed and replaced by a second cornice above it. Also, five windows of varied sizes that provided exterior light to the basement just below any former arched stained-glass windows have been sealed with matching grey concrete blocks.

Other exterior observations are seen as well. The door on the north front left side of the building was probably only a decorative entrance then as it is now. The second door on the front south side of the building seems to remain minimally unchanged from its original designs and function. The congregation's name and announcements signage were mounted on the west wall next to the right entrance of the building.

The building's square footage is about the same dimensions as the *Iglesia Bautista Del Salvador* with 3,000 square feet on the sanctuary floor and the same dimensions in the basement. The sanctuary can easily seat two hundred people. An over-flow semi-curved balcony exists but area around it has been repurposed for children's Christian education classes. Also, a small office and a walkway at the rear of this area allows people to reach the sanctuary or the basement area.

Sometime after 1988, I remember seeing the interior of the first-floor sanctuary area. The pews used by the former congregation had been removed, probably years ago by one of the occupants or owners of the building.

I surmise the pulpit from which the East Side United Methodist Church pastor preached was located on a raised floor along the room's west wall. The center of this wall may have contained a large stained-glass multi-sectional arched window discussed above. It brought in outside light which penetrated the colored glass that probably filled the sanctuary with artistic and thematic beauty. In this configuration, the preacher may have faced the congregation as they sat in pews on the main floor and the balcony area. The elimination of the large stained-glass window is seen in *Chicago's Southeast Side Cultural Institutions: A Community of Churches*. Today, a large sign of the name of the church covers this exterior wall area.

Methodists love to praise God through music. Therefore, I surmise there could have been rows of chairs on various levels on the pulpit where the choir probably sat. There must have been a pipe organ in the sanctuary that accompanied their congregational singing and used in their other services. The pastor's lectern could have been placed in the center of the pulpit in front of the choir, or to the left or right side. Without pictures and written information, we can only speculate as to the beauty that filled the pulpit and oak wood everywhere around it.

Since Community Christian Church of Chicago acquired the site, other interior and exterior modifications have been made costing thousands of dollars and hundreds of labor hours contributed by congregant volunteer's, and external contractors' leadership. In the interior, major and minor modifications have been made to facilitate activities, e.g., worship services, Christian education, administrative purposes, athletics, and other fellowship events.

The Community Christian Church of Chicago leaders introduced another major sanctuary modification. On the interior east wall area, a baptistry was installed high behind and above the small, raised pulpit. It is on the east side of the sanctuary from where the original may have been located on the west side. No stained-glass windows of any size or design are found in this room or in any part of the building.

The current interior redesign of the sanctuary has been executed in a traditional American Christian house of worship. The rectangular clear glass windows are encased in light-yellow oak wood shudders with light blue sheer curtains. This color motif is seen throughout the room. Aisles are found in the center and sides of the room. Several long octagonal chandeliers mounted to the ceiling and some wall sconce lights brightly illuminate the room. In 2022, the background of the pulpit was modified to enhance the on-line transmission of the services.

Other modern accoutrements have been added in the sanctuary. An in-house sound and word projection system with an unobtrusive control booth was installed at the back of the west wall of the sanctuary. For years, an ebony-colored grand piano was used by the congregation's early pianist, Hector Roque. His successor was a young congregant, David Díaz, who later used an electronic keyboard and lead singers during congregational singing.

Whenever I came to Chicago, I visited this church and was invited to accompany David on the piano. Between 2019-2023, when the COVID-19 pandemic was rampant, their services continued but with loss of attendance. Accompaniment and use of singers was modified by using guitar and prerecorded music sans piano or keyboard. This music model has been restored and varied to enhance the on-line transmission of their beautiful contemporary Sunday services.

This historic building was bought with a challenging accessibility issue in its 1914 construction design. This issue was the steep curving staircase people had to ascend in order to reach the sanctuary from the South Ewing Avenue entrance. The use of mechanical technology was the solution. The installation of a remote-controlled moving one-chair mounted to a curved steel rail was introduced between 2014-2017. This system facilitated accessibility to all who wished to worship in this House of prayer in addition to the wooden original stairway.

No whole-building air conditioning system seemed to be available until Community Christian Church Chicago installed one. It included a new heating and air-conditioning system around 2018-2019. A modern in-ceiling heating and cooling system with ducts and recessed lighting in the ceilings of the basement area has also been added. The latter was led under the direction of David Pérez, a skilled parishioner who was actively involved in several construction solutions in the building. A doorway on the east wall of the basement allows people to access the stairway to enter the sanctuary upstairs.

This stairway also provides access through a small vestibule near a south exit from the building. Along the way this stairway passes a small men's restroom. Another micro-restroom for men is also found in the basement near the west wall. In addition, a small classroom is located in the north wall area of the basement near the west staired entry to this room.

A doorway in the middle of the sanctuary's south wall leads to a stairway. At the terminus is a small, modern kitchen found in the east portion of the basement in which wonderful Latino and other cuisine dishes are prepared by congregation women. A women's restroom is located on the south wall of the main floor. A vestibule is located at the rear of the sanctuary's double-door entryway where a stairway leads to a classroom space in the balcony area.

Another major expense to the congregation was considered and incurred a short time after acquiring the building. Some fifty thousand dollars were spent to restore and modify the structure and redesign the interior and exterior sections that needed attention. This expense may have been above the others incurred upon buying the property and modifying it as said earlier. Nonetheless, these expenses were embraced by the members as its own second house of worship since it moved out of their first building in Jeffery Manor years earlier.

On June 25, 1989, a Dedication Service was held. It started before 9:00 a.m. and ran into the afternoon hours. The sanctuary was filled with parishioners and visitors. They came to memorialize how God's spiritual guidance, the congregation's unwavering faith, their physical and financial contribution, brought them to this milestone.

The Sanctuary of Community Christian Church of Chicago when it was dedicated, Sunday, June 25, 1989. The pulpit has been modified to complement its worship services. The baptistry is directly above the pulpit. (Source: Dedication Service, 1989.)

The program was a solemn event. Holy Communion service was celebrated. Deacon John Rivera led a Special Presentation. Brother Robert Sloniger, Executive Director of the then Chicago District Evangelistic Association led the reading of the Act of Dedication. Lydia Rivera, my sister-in law and long-time church secretary aurally presented brief histories of three previous pastors and the current one. The program listed the names of five elders and seven deacons. A review of the chronology and major milestones since 1960 when this church began which brought them to this dedication is provided in the program. Acknowledgement was expressed to external professional businesses and individuals that provided specialized personal services which helped the congregation move forward through the years.

Pastor Ricardo Ayala delivered a message in English and Spanish. A meaningful Bible reference for the event was used from the Old Testament Book written by the Prophet Isaiah, Chapter 40, Verse 31:

"But they that wait upon the Lord shall renew their strength, they shall mount up with wings as eagles, they shall run and not be weary, and they shall walk and not faint."

This encouraging Bible passage was a regular expression which millions of listeners heard Rev. Dr. Robert Schuller pronounce during the Sunday morning services at the former Crystal Cathedral in Anaheim, California which were broadcast on television during his twenty-year tenure here.

As the congregation continued to grow in its ministry, in 2011, it elected a young man to be their full-time Pastor, Eliezer De León, from the Latin American nation of the Dominican Republic, in the Caribbean Island of Hispañola. He is bilingual in Spanish and English, which complements the congregation's needs to spread the gospel in the greater area. He eagerly and effectively continues as to serve as their pastor in 2023, accompanied by his wife, Amanda Ruck De León, who is originally hails from Michigan, and their young four young children, Neftalí, Daniel, Leora, and Elena.

Pastor De León is in his thirteenth year as full-time pastor of this congregation. His special distinction is that he is the son of a pastor from his homeland. During the sixty-four years existence of this congregation (1960-2024), each full-time pastor has served an average of ten years which is remarkable, especially for a small bilingual Spanish-speaking congregation in South Chicago. This church started with a small number of members supporting this Christian effort. In 2023, membership is approximately 150 people with a healthy potential of reaching others for Christ in the future years.

Throughout its history, this congregation has brought the Word to all people via a myriad of venues beyond. These include their homes, parks, other rented church sites and their other campus property adjacent to their building. The alfresco Easter Sunday service was held for years at daybreak near Calumet Park's New Beach along Lake Michigan's shoreline just north of the U.S. Coast Guard Station. Worshippers wrapped themselves in blankets and sat in the brisk morning air on large limestone blocks to hear the message of the resurrection of Christ and of its significance to mankind. The COVID-19 pandemic caused the cancellation of this very early morning activity for three years until Easter 2023 when it was reinstated.

The Easter worship service was generally led by the late John B. Rivera, son of Juan Bautista Rivera (John B), my brother-in-law, and father-in-law, respectively. A typical image of the 1987 pre-dawn service is found in the photograph[94] provided by Rita Arias Jirasek and Carlos Tortolero's book, *Images of America: Mexican Chicago*. Both of these writers are former Bowen High School teachers who continue to be involved in other community activities today.

Growth also brought a challenge to worshipers for parking their cars. Public street parking was insufficient and inadequate in this residential community. This issue was partially resolved when the congregation purchased an empty lot north of its building at the corner of 133rd Street and South Ewing Avenue.

During 2018-2019, the congregation bought a wooden residential structure immediately adjacent to the north side of the building for several thousand dollars. As the building was deemed too costly to renovate and make useful to meet the congregation's needs, it was razed and repurposed for convenient additional parking spaces. In addition, this area is used for celebrating year-round activities for all ages including a garden to grow flowers and other small plants.

The congregation also has plans to add and expand selective activities to their current indoor and outdoor Christian education and athletic programs. These have been held in a brick building which the congregation acquired in the recent past. It is located just east of their major property, across the public alley.

It was a house of worship for another Christian congregation that closed its doors when its membership declined as the community's demographics changed and as its congregants moved away. It needed but could not find leadership to continue an effective ministry. Some of the impacted members of the former congregation visited the Christian Community Church of Chicago and several of them became members who wished to worship God and serve with their new brothers and sisters in their familiar neighborhood.

When the East Side United Methodist Church completed their building in 1914, they embedded in large Gothic letters in the middle of the façade a phrase that has endured for 110 years. Passersby could readily see it for years and is still observable today: *"TO THE GLORY OF GOD."* In the recent past, these words received a new coat of gold colored paint to emphasize and highlight their presence. In 2022-2023, a beautiful and attractive large sign with the full name of the congregation was mounted on the façade of the building just below the original expression.

Today, the embedded words remain a living public affirmation by the dedicated servant-leader members of The Community Christian Church of Chicago. They continue to lead people to fulfill their spiritual and other needs. This body has served the community from this site for the last twenty-eight out of its sixty-four years since it was founded. With God's blessing, and Christ's and the Holy Spirit's indwelling, the ministry of this congregation will prevail for years to come...to the glory of God.

EPILOGUE

The effort to research the history of the First Baptist Church of South Chicago since its founding in 1879 has been a challenge[95]. While much information is scarce, I have attempted to share my work in this book believing that more history has yet to be discovered. The information I present has been invaluable to learning about how and when the English-speaking Baptist congregation facilitated the establishment of the Mexican Baptist congregation in an old wooden structure in 1926 three years before The Great Depression started worldwide.

I am fortunate to have been able to find documentation which I gleaned over years from various sources. I derived printed material from my personal files, parishioners, pastors, and descendants of those who worshipped and served in *Iglesia Bautista Del Salvador* from its founding until it closed sixty-five years later. I present this narrative in the hope that it will advance the history about the English and Spanish-speaking Baptists and their work in South Chicago. They were unflinching Christian here and in other states and communities.

Some members of *Iglesia Bautista Del Salvador* congregation are linked to the history, founding and growth of a new congregation, Community Christian Church of Chicago which sprouted in 1960. Our interlaced lives provide an example and understanding of how God produced a fruitful outcome for His Kingdom.

The Spanish-speaking cohort will continue to grow to serve God and reach people to share the Word. This will be as Christians, Baptists, other Evangelical Protestant denominations and as Roman Catholics. Each group brought the Word to Ainsworth, its founding name in 1833 and later South Chicago by immigrants.

Notes About The Author

GEORGE BÉLOZ[96] was born in South Chicago, lived most of his early life here and was a member of Iglesia Bautista Del Salvador. He earned a Ph.D., served as a diplomat and international relations officer with the U.S. State Department/U.S. Agency for International Development, and was an administrator in Higher Education. He resides in Southern California with his family.

ABBREVIATIONS USED IN NOTES[97]

ACM	*Alianza Cristiana y Misionera, Himnos de la Vida Cristian.* New York: 1939.
AM	Adam Morales, *American Baptist With a Spanish Accent.* The Judson Press: Valley Forge Pennsylvania, 1964.
BH	*Breve Historia De La Convención Bautista Hispano-Americana y Constitución De La Misma.* Rev. E.L. Balderas, Imprenta Bautista, East Chicago, Indiana, 1966. (Founded in 1928.)
CBC	Compassionate Church, *Who We Are.* Website. Chicago, Illinois:2021.
CBH	Coldwell Banker Homes. Chicago, 9001-south-houston-ave, December 5, 2019.
CDP	*Chicago Data Portal. Building Footprints Deprecated.* Chicago, 2015.
CFMC	*Chicago's First Mexican Church.* https://ineteractive.wttw.com/playlist/2017/09/20/chicago's-first-mexican-church.
CLCD	*Chicago Lakeside City Directory of Churches* of 1900
CH	*Celebration Hymnal,* Foreword, *Songs and Hymns for Worship.* Word Music/Integrity, USA, 1997
CS	*Chicano Settlements: A Brief History.* Louise Año Nuevo de Kerr, *in Journal of Ethnic Studies, 2,4, Winter, 1975.*
CLCD	*Chicago Lakeside City Directory.*
CSECI	*Chicago's Southeast Side Cultural Institutions (*See Bibliography.)
CT	*Chicago Tribune.*
DC	*Daily Calumet.*
DJB	Deborah J. Baldwin, *Protestants, and the Mexican Revolution: Missionaries, Ministers and Social Change.* University of Illinois Press. Champaign, Illinois, 1990.
DJG	John M. Gillette, *The Cultural Agencies of a Typical Manufacturing Group: South Chicago, Illinois, in American Journal of Sociology,* 1901, Volume 7, 2.
DT	*Daily Times.*
EL	*El Maná. Official Publication of Convención Bautista Hispano-Americana, , 1974, 1981, 1986.*
ES	*Evening Star.*
GB	George Béloz (See Bibliography.)
HLP	Harold L. Platt, *The Electric City,* Dissertation. University of Michigan, 1991.
HVC	*Himnos de la Vida Cristiana.* Alianza Cristiana y Misionera, Ninth Edition, New York.
IA	*Images of America.* (See Bibliography.)
IBR	*Illinois Baptist Review.*
IO	*Inter-Ocean Newspaper.* February 12, 1885; September 19, 1885. Chicago.
JH	James Huenink, *History Chicago Lutheran Church (South Chicago), 1873,* <hueninkwritersmedium.com>

JISH	*Journal of Illinois State History. Historical Society. Illinois' Oldest Memorial: The Stephen A. Douglas Monument.* 51, 2,Summer,1958. Also, www.nbchicago.com/news/local/stephen-a-douglas-statue-removed-from-Illinois-capital-lawn.
JPR	Jack Paul Rocha, *South Chicago Neighborhood House, Part One, in Southeast Chicago Historical Society News*, April 2022, Vol. XXXVI, Number 2.
MIJ	Michael Innis-Jiménez. (See Bibliography.)
NL	Newberry Library. Chicago.
NM	*Nuestro Magazine.* Reprint, 2. *New York:* April 1982.
RH	*Reseñas Históricas, Anniversary Program, Fifty-Third Year, 1926-1979.* Chicago: 1979.
RODS	Rod Sellers.
RS	Letter to Rev. Ralph Sanderson, Merrill Avenue Baptist Church. Chicago: July 14, 1964.
SCBR	*South Chicago Baptist Review, Thanksgiving Issue*, B-439-4. Chicago, November 1928.
SFIM	Sanborn Fire Insurance. Map, 72, 1897.
SM	St. Michael Archangel Catholic Church. Wikipedia, 2021, Chicago, Illinois.
SOF	*Spires of Faith.* (See Bibliography.)
TD	Théodore Dubois. (See Bibliography.)
THH	Tremont House Hotel. Chicago, https://en.wikipedia.org/wiki/raising_of_chicago, p.7.
TP	*Times-Pacyune.* New Orleans, Louisiana. January: 1911.
WM	William Martin Study, *House Street Name Changes*. Chicago, 1948.
YS	*Youth Sings: A Praise Book of Hymns and Choruses.* Praise Book Publications, Mound, Minnesota: 1951.

NOTES

[1] Dedication.
[2] CBC Website, "Who We Are" February 2021.
[3] Acknowledgements.
[4] Introduction.
[5] Part I: First Baptist Church of South Chicago.
[6] IO, 7.https://.newspapers.com, Chicago. September 19, 1885, 15.
[7] CT, September 28, 1885, 5-6.
[8] SCBR, Chicago, 1928.
[9] Ibid, October 1929.
[10] IBR, Vol. XXIII, Joliet, June 1932.
[11] DT, Jan 13, 1931.
[12] RG.
[13] DJG, "The Cultural Sources of a Typical Manufacturing Group: South Chicago Illinois, American Journal of Sociology, Vol. 7, #2, 1901.
[14] RS, letter by Marguerite Everham to Rev. R. Sanderson, July 24, 1964.
[15] NM, Reprint, "Trouble in the Bush," April 1982, 2.
[16] JPR, Southeast Chicago Historical Society News, April 2022, Newsletter, C. Mulac, Editor, Vol, XXVI, Number 2.
[17] CT, http://Chicagotribune.newspaper.com. Tuesday, July 15,1897.
[18] GB, 2018.
[19] DC, Chicago, Monday, February 2, 1953,1.
[20] Ibid.
[21] Ibid.
[22] ES, Saturday, August 30, Washington, D.C., 1902, 4.
[23] CLCD, ill/cook/churches Geneaologytrails.com/1900, 3.
[24] DC, Chicago, Monday, February 2, 1953,1.
[25] Ibid.
[26] CSECI.
[27] CFMC.
[28] SOF (see Bibliography).
[29] Part II: First Mexican Baptist Church of South Chicago (1926).
[30] CSECI.
[31] RODS, e-mail, February 25, 2021.
[32] RH, ibid.
[33] RH, ibid.

[34] RH, ibid.
[35] Part III: Mexicans Purchase the Baptist Building, And Its Ministry (1953).
[36] IO, Ibid.
[37] SANB, https://www.loc.gov/resourced/g4104cm.g017901897FImage-40SanbornFireIns.map. Chicago, Cook County, Illinois, 10-14.
[38] WM, chsmedia.org/househistory/Namechanges/start.pdf. William Martin, chgo, 1948.
[39] CBH, https://www.coldwellbankershouses.com/il (chicago)9001-houston.ave/p.d.Dec5,2019.
[40] CDP, (also, deprecated), 2020. 46 "when electricity arrived" HLP.
[41] THH.
[42] CT, Arthur Pollard, "Paving of Streets Requires 12-Foot Stone Wall." 194211025p41.streetsartcl.jpg, in CSSCI files.
[43] New Owners, Old Challenges.
[44] Membership Directories.
[45] Three Additional Land Parcels Bought.
[46] Building Signage.
[47] Interior Beautification.
[48] Interior Description.
[49] Entrance View.
[50] The Sanctuary Pulpit.
[51] Holy Communion Sacrament.
[52] Baptism Sacrament.
[53] Music in the Services.
[54] CH, Foreword.
[55] Christian Education.
[56] Sunday Morning Worship Service.
[57] Sunday Evening Worship Service.
[58] https://en.wikipedia.org/wiki/Queen_of_the_Night_aria
[59] Wednesday Evening Services.
[60] Additional Christian Education.
[61] Special Music Programs.
[62] HVC.
[63] HVC.
[64] A Good Friday Cantata.
[65] TD.
[66] CT, March 28, 1964.
[67] Other Choir Programs.
[68] Children in Music and Dramas.

[69] Beauty in Historic Houses of God.
[70] SM.
[71] MIJ.
[72] Mexican Immigrants Choose South Chicago.
[73] Part IV: Leadership and Development.
[74] Ibid., 20.
[75] Ibid., 23.
[76] Ibid., 31.
[77] Ibid., 32.
[78] Ibid., 23.
[79] Ibid., 23.
[80] Ibid., 21.
[81] Ibid., 21.
[82] JMG, 202. MIJ, op. cit., 84.
[83] DJG, 19.
[84] AM, 70-75.
[85] Hispanic Leadership Recognition.
[86] AM, 70-75.
[87] EM.
[88] Hispanic Baptist Conventions And Associations.
[89] Presidents of the Hispanic Conventions and Associations (1928-1978).
[90] Youth Activities.
[91] YS.
[92] Part V: Founding of the Community Christian Church South Chicago (1960).
[93] A Permanent Building Is Found" (1988).
[94] IA (See Bibliography), 108.
[95] Epilogue.
[96] Notes About The Author.
[97] Abbreviations Used in Notes.

BIBLIOGRAPHY

Arias Jirasek, Rita, Carlos Tortolero, and Book Project Manager, Linda Xochitl Tortolero López. *Mexican Chicago, Images of America*. Arcadia Publishing, an Imprint of Tempus Publishing, Inc., Chicago. 2001.

Béloz, George. *Colonel James Harvey Bowen: The Epic of His Life and South Chicago's First High School Centennial Celebration*, Fifth Edition, Corona, California, 2018.

Chicago's Southeast Side Cultural Institutions: A Community of Churches. Washington High School, Chicago. Museology Class. Rod Sellers, coordinator. Southeast Historical Museum, Calumet Park. Chicago. 2001-2002.

Dubois, Theódore. *The Seven Last Words of Christ*, G. Schermer, Inc., New York, 1899.

de Kerr, Louise Año Nuevo, *Chicano Settlements in Chicago: A Brief History, Journal of Ethnic Studies, 2,4, Winter, 1975*.

Gillettte, John Morris. *The Culture Agencies of a Typical Manufacturing Group: South Chicago, Illinois*. The University of Chicago Press, *American Journal of Sociology*, Vol. 7, 2, 1901.

Innis-Jiménez. Michael, *Steel Barrio: The Great Mexican Migration to South Chicago, 1915-1940*. New York University Press. 2013.

Morales, Adam. *Baptist With a Spanish Accent*. The Judson Press, Valley Forge, Pennsylvania, 1964.

Wolf, Wayne, Jack Simmerling, and Miriam Kravis. *Spires of Faith, Historic Churches of Chicago*. McGraw-Hill, Inc., 1995.

MEMBERS AND VETERANS OF
IGLESIA BAUTISTA DEL SALVADOR

This roster of seventy-nine family names is compiled from Church Directories printed in 1965, 1966, and 1974. Many passive and earlier ones were not available for use therefore their names are not listed though we remember them.

The family husband's and wife's first names are provided. Single surnames and first names are also shown in some entries. Children's names are not included though we know some of the families had up to six.

Seven former pastors during the above years were also members of this congregation. Their names are listed on the roster of pastors of this church.

The 40th Anniversary of this church in 1966 lists the names of three of our young men who were active in the United States Armed Forces. They were Romeo D. Muñoz (Army) in Viet Nam, Genaro Quinoñes (Marines), and Ralph Quinoñes (Air Force). Each veteran returned home and brought our congregation a sense of pride. The two Quiñones servicemen were sons of Cruz and Georgina Quiñones. Romeo was the son of Rev. Pilar and Isabel Muñoz. I had already served in the Army (1961-1963).

Alcalá, Jesús & Mercedes
Apolinar, Silvestre & María
Armas, Felipe & Severina
Armas, Lidia
Armendáriz, Crestino & Antoniette
Aseves, Aurelio & Élida
Autry, Lawrence
Báez, Ramón & Ramona
Barrón, Manuel & Armandina
Bautista, Aristeo & Catalina
Béloz, George & Ruth
Béloz, Protascio & Kathlene
Barreto, Ernestina
Briones, Antonio & Florinda
Briones, Salvador & Carmen
Casas, Pedro & Luisa
Cendejas, Francisco & Celestina
Dávila, Refugio & María
De La Paz, Jesús & María
De Hoyos, Diana
Días, Agustín & Consuelo
Estévez, Samuel & Anita
Evans, Luis & Carmen
Fierro, Jesús & Dolores
Fierro, Jonathan & Anita
Flores, Herminia
Flores, Rubén & Agapita
Galarza, Celia

Gaona, Peter & María Elvira
García, Natividad & Francisca
Garza, Manuel & Sylvia
González, Jesús & Adela
González, Paul & Kathleen
Hermida, Milca
López, Genaro & Justina
López, Juan & Marcelina
López, Rev. Moisés & Guadalupe
Luera, Erineo
Macías, Federico & Rosa María
Manzo, Ramiro & Dolores
Martínez, Daniel & Mary
Martínez, Ramón & Mary
Mata, Francisco & María
Mendoza, José & Ángela
Montemayor, Daniel & Patricia
Montemayor, Tomás & Esther
Morales, Rosalinda
Muñoz, Rev. Pilar & Isabel
Muñoz, Roldán & Dorothy
Norad, Gladys
Ozuna, Rev. Domingo & Dolores
Pérez, Antonio & Rhoda
Pérez, Francisco & Elisa
Pérez, Oswaldo & Rebeca
Pérez, Sebastían & Ángela

Piedra, Rafael
Puerta, Joaquín & Juanita
Quiñones, Cruz & Georgina
Quiñones, Ralph & Carmen
Ramírez, Benny & Mary
Ramirez, Ray & Rebeca
Reyes, Santiago & Benita
Ricardi, Héctor
Ríos, David & Carolyn
Robles, Frank & Eunice
Rodríguez, Carlos
Rodríguez, Olivia
Rodríguez, Saúl & Angelita
Rucoba, Rodolfo & Lidia
Ruíz, Pedro & Belén
Salinas, Rev. Humberto & Socorro
Torres, Luis & Guadalupe
Trinidad, Reyes & Rafaela
Vargas, Jorge & Theresa
Vázquez, Alberto & María
Vázquez, Albino & Elisa
Velasco, Michael & Pámela
Villareal, Arturo & Anastacia
Williams, Richard & Laura

INDEX

Aceves, Élida, 99, 101
Adesanya, Emmanuel Soji, 69
Agudath Achim Bikur Cholim Synagogue, 43, 68
Alvarado, Armando M., 50, 164
American Baptist Convention, 47, 157, 162
American Baptist Home Mission Societies, 47, 155
Apolinar, Susie. (See Wells)
Aposento Alto, 92
Araujo, Pastor Marcelo, 78
Arias Jirasek, Rita, 189, 199
Armas, Lydia (Lee), 101, 124, 131, 133, 144, 171, 201
Asociación Bautista Lagunera, 165, 166, 167, 168, 169
Ayala, Ricardo, 180, 181, 188
Badaracco, Dino, 168
Balderas
    Amelia, 9, 50, 95, 157
    Efraín, 9, 50, 51, 83, 84, 142, 157, 162, 163, 164, 166, 168, 170, 193
    Terri Thomas, 157
Baldwin, Deborah, 152, 193
Baptist Missionary Training School, 15, 158
Baptist Review, 20, 193, 194
Bautista
    Aristeo and Catalina, 120
    Isaiah, 120
Béloz
    Augustine, 120

Carmen, 120
Cheryl, 9
Janet Stewart, 9
Peter, 131, 133
Protascio, 201
Ruth, 9, 133
Berry, Marvin, 51, 52, 54
Bird Memorial Center, 61
Blasko, Sarah Montemayor, 9
Bowen High School, 27, 28, 56, 59, 121, 127, 128, 129, 173, 189
Bowen, Colonel James Harvey, 23, 24, 26, 28
Boyd, Dr., 34
Bratton, Ralph, 51, 54, 166
Breve Historia De La Convención Hispano-Americana, Y Constitución De La Misma (1928-1965), 99, 100, 101, 102, 162, 163, 164, 168, 169, 193
Briones, Moisés, 107
Brown, Joseph H. Steel Company, 18, 24
Bush Neighborhood, 23, 140, 158, 179
Buzo, Sarita, 163
Calumet & Chicago Canal & Dock Company, 26, 68
Calumet Park, 21, 28, 38, 189, 199
Carnegie Steel Mill. (See South Works)
Casa Central, 135

Castillo, Miguel, 100, 163, 164, 166, 169, 170
Chicago Data Portal, 62, 193
Chicago District Evangelical Assn., 136
Chicago Street Changes, 58
Chicago Tribune, 17, 18, 24, 26, 66, 132, 193
Chicago's Southeast Side Industrial History, 25
Chicago's Southeast Side Cultural Institutions, 182
Chickering Piano, 89, 99, 110, 120, 185
Coldwater Banker, 79
Colonel James Harvey Bowen, 59, 199
Commercial Avenue, 27, 28, 41, 61, 64, 72, 73
Community Christian Church of Chicago, 11, 142, 180, 181, 182, 184, 187, 190, 191
Compassion Baptist Church of Chicago, 34, 37, 101
Daily Calumet, 36, 193
Daily Times, 21, 193
De León, Eliezer and Amanda, 188
Díaz, David, 185
Directorio De La Iglesia Bautista El Salvador, 83
Douglas, Steven, 145, 194
Durik, Pedro, 50, 53, 54
Echevarría, Raúl, 50
El Maná, 155, 163, 193
Emmanuel Lutheran Church, 60
Estéviz, Anita, 133

Fierro
  Anita Sasso, 99, 121, 130, 133, 144, 158, 159
  Dolores, Jesús & Jonathan, 103, 158
First Baptist Church of South Chicago
  built, 11, 22, 56, 96
  chartered, 15, 33
  dedicated, 17, 36, 47
  sold to Mexicans, 7, 11, 46, 57
First University of Chicago, 15
Fontañez, F. Soto, 135
Founding of the Mexican Mission, 49, 160
Fourth Baptist Church, Chicago, 17
Fugitive, The, 63
Galindo, Félix T., 48, 163
García, Víctor, 48, 49, 50
Garza, Ranulfo, 178
Gillette, John M., 22, 23, 152, 193
Gonsález
  Adela, 93, 103, 133
  Jesús, 19, 93, 102
  Paul, 112, 124, 173
Great Cities Institute, 64
Griesel, Adam, 20
Gurrola
  Carlos M., 48, 49, 50, 102, 153, 154
  Photo, https //convencbautista.com.rev_ carlos, 102
Hanchuck, Eugenio, 129
Hegewisch, 28, 61, 179
Huenink, James, 68, 193

Iglesia Bautista Del Salvador, 7, 9, 11, 12, 13, 18, 28, 32, 38, 44, 45, 50, 55, 57, 58, 67, 69, 77, 78, 79, 82, 85, 86, 88, 91, 92, 94, 98, 101, 104, 106, 108, 109, 110, 112, 113, 114, 122, 123, 124, 128, 129, 135, 136, 138, 140, 142, 147, 148, 153, 154, 155, 156, 157, 158, 159, 161,164, 166, 168, 171, 174, 177, 179, 180, 183, 191, 192

Iglesia La Luz Del Mundo, 62, 64, 65, 67, 75, 77, 78, 79, 81, 82, 88, 90, 94, 97, 99, 104, 107, 108

Illinois Baptist Bulletin, 21

Images of America
    Mexican Chicago, 189

Immaculate Conception Catholic Church, 41

Innis-Jiménez, Michael, 144, 145, 148, 152, 194, 199

Inter Ocean, 16, 17, 55

Jeffery Manor Community Christian Church, 178, 180

Jiménez, Carlos, 50

Jones, Watson III, 34, 37

Journal of Illinois State History, 194

Junco Gonsález, Juan, 50

Kelly, A.C., 22, 30

Kennard, Rev. Dr., 17

Kerr, Louise, 144, 193, 199

La Asociación Ministerial Hispana, 134, 135

Latin Youth for Christ, 172, 173

Lockhart, Dinah (Pérez), and Jerry, 112

Loera, Isaías Hernández, 164

Long, Rev., 20, 21

López
    Daniel M., 129, 173
    Moisés G., 45, 50

Macías, Rev. Jim, 100, 164

Magaña
    Daniel, 153
    David, 122
    Sara Hernández, 121, 124, 129

Maizteguí, Father John, 40

Manzo, Dolores and Ramiro, 100, 101, 103, 201

Marcano, Martha López, 101, 115, 171

Mardirosián, Vahac, 164

Martin, William, 58, 194, 196

Martínez
    Henry, 179, 180
    Mary, 9, 95, 100, 101, 103, 126, 133, 156, 158, 162
    Ramón, 9, 95, 156
    Steve, 179
    Theresa, 9, 93, 95, 103, 157

Mascareñas, Cesar O., 51, 155, 164

McNeil, J. W. T., 34

Merrill Avenue Baptist Church, 36, 37, 194

Mexican tri-state representation, 148

Mohoney, A. A., 34

Montemayor
    Esther, 103, 159
    Lydia Rucoba, 159

Sarah Blasko, 9
Tomás, 50, 159, 164, 201
Moody Bible Institute, 20, 181
Morales
    Adam, 153, 154, 155, 164, 167, 193
    Benjamín, 155
Morán, Cheryl Béloz, 9
Mulcahy, Elena Berezaluce, 180
Muñoz
    Isabel, 159, 161, 171, 201
    Rev. Pilar, 45, 50, 51, 52, 53, 54, 83, 84, 86, 102, 156, 159, 160, 161, 164
    Rhoda, 112, 160, 201
    Roby, 100
    Romeo, 201
Muñoz Becerra, Rev. Jacinto, 50
New Holy Trinity Temple, 79, 88
North Chicago Rolling Mill Company, 24
Northern Baptist Convention, 21
NUESTRO Magazine, 23, 174
O'Neal, Ken, 38
Odell, D.D., 17, 22, 30
Our Lady of Guadalupe Catholic Church, 39
Ozuna
    Dolores, 50, 86, 102, 103, 201
    Domingo, 50, 86, 102, 201
Paderewski, Ignace Jan, 141
Pérez
    Ángela Briones and Sebastián, 107
    Antonio, 52, 112, 160, 161
    David, 104, 185

Dinah, 112, 156, 160, 161, (Also see Lockhart)
Elisa, 9, 104, 137, 158, 201
Frank, 52, 95, 104, 137, 158
John, 160
Marcus, 160
Raúl, 137
Rhoda, 112, 160, 201, (Also see Muñoz)
Pilgrim Baptist Church, 43
Podkul, Joann, 38
Pollard, Arthur, 72, 73, 196
Potter, Orrin W., 24
Primera Iglesia Bautista El Salvador, 7
Primera Iglesia Bautista Mexicana de Sur Chicago, 7, 44
Primera Iglesia Bautista Mexicana El Salvador, 48, 162
Primitive Christian Church, 79, 88
Pullman, George, 71, 72
Quiñones
    Cruz, 201
    Genaro, 201
    Georgina, 201
    Ralph, 112
Raising Streets, 56, 71, 72, 74
Reseñas Históricas, 46, 47, 48, 177, 194
Rivera
    Ignacia, 103, 178
    John B., 189
    Juan Bautista, 166, 178, 189
    Lydia, 180, 187
    Ruth N., 133, (Also see Béloz)
Rocha, Jack Paul, 23, 194

Rucoba, Lydia Montemayor, 159, 201
Ruíz, Pedro and Belén, 52, 90
Saint Jude Shrine, 40
Saint Michael Archangel Roman Catholic Church, 41, 138, 139, 141
Salinas
   Benjamín, 101, 137
   Humberto, 50, 53, 83, 84, 85, 86, 101, 102, 133, 164
   Nehemías, 101
   Socorro, 101, 137, 201
Sanborn Fire Insurance Map (Library of Congress www.loc.gov/resource/g4104cm.g017901897F/), 31, 56, 57
Sanderson, Ralph, 23, 194, 195
Santiago, Florencio, 48, 49, 153, 163, 164
Schuller, Robert, 188
Sellers, Rod, 25, 34, 38, 194, 199
Sheridan, Philip Henry, 28, 59
Short, Jeff E., 50, 51, 52, 54
Signage, 87, 88, 183
Sloniger, Robert, 187
Snyder, Mario O., 135, 172
Soledad, José, 48, 171
South Chicago Masonic Temple, 47, 179
South Chicago Neighborhood House, 15, 23, 36, 47, 123, 159, 179, 194
South Works, 24, 25, 146

Southeast Chicago Historical Society, 21, 23, 28, 38, 96, 182, 195
Southern Baptist Association, 85
Spanish American Baptist Seminary, 48
Spires of Faith, 40, 194, 199
Steel Barrio. (See Innis-Jiménez)
Streetscape Design Guidelines, 61
Sullivan, William K. Elementary School, 140
Swedish Bethany Lutheran Church, 43
Thomas, Terri. (See Balderas)
Thome, Jacobo A., 100, 164
Thompson, Henry, 33, 34, 35, 36, 37
Thorp, J. N., 28, 59
Tortolero, Carlos, 189, 199
Tremont House Hotel, 71, 194
U.S. Steel Corporation, 25
Union Park Congregational Church, 138, 139, 140
Urbina, Susie, 78
Villagrana, Francisco, 48, 171
Vreeland, C. F., 34, 35
Wells, Susie and William, 144, 159
Williams, Basil, 36, 48, 101
Woolhouse, Edgar, 33, 48, 171
Young, Albert, 178
Youth Sings, A Praise Book, 172
Zion Lutheran Church, 43